Labrador Nurse

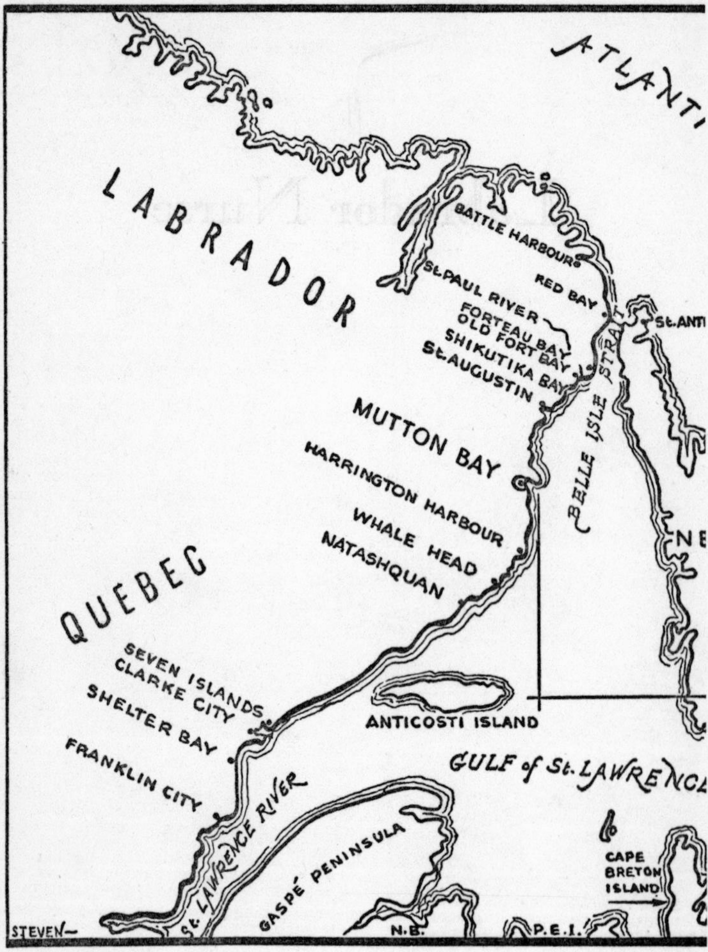

ATLANTI
LABRADOR
BATTLE HARBOUR
RED BAY
St. PAUL RIVER
FORTEAU BAY
OLD FORT BAY
SHIKUTIKA BAY
St. AUGUSTIN
St. ANTI
MUTTON BAY
HARRINGTON HARBOUR
WHALE HEAD
NATASHQUAN
BELLE ISLE STRAIT
NE
QUEBEC
SEVEN ISLANDS
CLARKE CITY
SHELTER BAY
FRANKLIN CITY
ANTICOSTI ISLAND
GULF of St. LAWRENCE
St. LAWRENCE RIVER
GASPÉ PENINSULA
CAPE BRETON ISLAND
N.B.
P.E.I.
STEVEN

LABRADOR NURSE

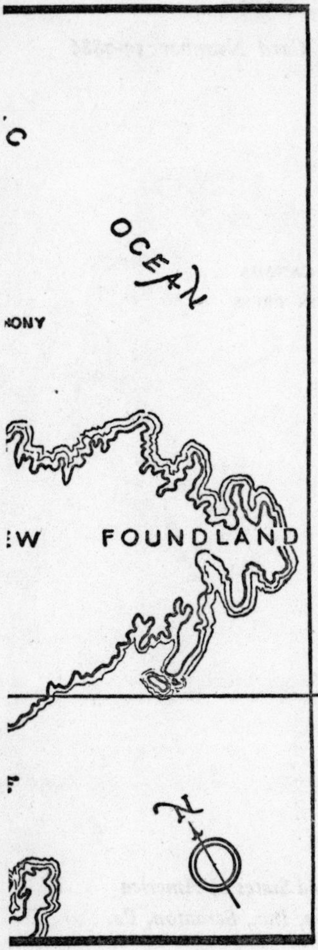

B. J. Banfill

MACRAE SMITH COMPANY

PHILADELPHIA

Library of Congress Catalog Card Number 53-7886

PUBLISHED IN CANADA
BY THE RYERSON PRESS

538

Manufactured in the United States of America
By The Haddon Craftsmen, Inc., Scranton, Pa.

Introduction

"THE land God gave to Cain . . . not a cartload of earth on the whole of it." Thus Jacques Cartier described the Labrador Coast in 1534.

This rocky shore was apparently unknown to the Western world until the end of the tenth century. Leif Ericson, who saw it about 1000, called it *Helluland* or *Flat Stone Land*. John Cabot, nearly 500 years later, mentioned the great numbers of codfish he saw off the coast; records show that whalers and sealers have long frequented Labrador waters. But most navigators were disappointed in the land and sailed away—Frobisher in 1577, Davis in 1586, and Knight in 1606.

France became interested in Labrador when such men as Bourbon and Jolliet saw it in the seventeenth century. *La Compagnie des Indes* granted Francois Bissot, a Norman immigrant, the land and fishing rights over a district extending from Seven Isles to Bradore Bay. He was the first Canadian to tan leather and also established the first seal fisheries in the Gulf.

Labrador has changed hands many times. Under the French it was part of Canada. When Canada became a British colony in 1763, Labrador and Anticosti were annexed to Newfoundland. In 1774 Labrador was given back to Canada and in 1809 it was reannexed to Newfoundland. The boundaries had always been loosely defined, but in 1927 Privy Council decreed that the eastern part of Labrador, which borders on the Atlantic Coast, was part of Newfoundland. This is what for many years was Canadian Labrador. All of Labrador is now under the jurisdiction of the Canadian government, since Newfoundland became the tenth province of Canada in 1950.

I was attracted to this cold, uninviting land by the Grenfell Mission Stations and Hospital along the Atlantic Coast. As a nurse connected with the Mission, I was glad to serve the scattered hamlets of fishermen who wrested a precarious living from the sea. Their need for nursing and medical service was great.

In the narrative that follows, some of the place names and, for obvious reasons, most of the personal names, are fictitious. I have attempted to give an unprejudiced picture of the lives of these hardy, brave fisherfolk, whom I greatly admire. I lived and worked with them first in 1928 and later in 1942, during the Second World War, when living conditions were very much better.

part one: 1928

THERE'S the pier, and there's the boat!" exclaimed my taxi driver as he jolted to a stop at the Quebec docks. I paid my fare, adjusted my heavy coat on one arm, my raincoat on the other, seized both bags, and made my way over the scorching cinders to Pier Two.

"Where to, ma'am?" briskly enquired a steward at the pier's end.

"Mutton Bay."

"Right you are. Follow me."

I mounted the forty-five degree angle gangplank behind him,

high-stepped the footboards on the deck, ducked under the low-ceilinged door beams, then dived into the depths below. The steward opened the door of a cabin and put my bags inside.

"Take your choice, ma'am—upper or lower. You are first in. We leave at four o'clock."

I was lucky to have first choice. A lower berth did not require a ladder. Fresh, damp salt air generously supplied the upper, but since the ventilator was the only porthole, during a storm it could be a menace, unexpectedly showering the upper inmate with icy, salt water. The lower was more spacious and convenient, but one had to take everything into consideration.

I chose a lower and later regretted the lack of fresh air but, dry and unscathed, rejoiced with each morning's security no matter how stormy the night had been.

I had time to examine at leisure this stout little *North Shore*, which was so much a part of life at Mutton Bay. The ship was evidently not built for comfort or beauty but for service and safety. From the captain's lookout on the upper deck to the lowest inch on the water-drawing line, the *North Shore* was fashioned to battle the wildest and roughest seas and to carry essential cargo.

On deck all seemed confusion: yapping melancholy-looking dogs, piles of lumber, drums of gasoline, miles of galvanized pipe, empty fish cases, huge coils of hempen rope. In stormy seas, I later learned, this cargo was apt to scuttle back and forth as the boat lurched and tossed.

Gaping, mammoth hatches, aft and stern, were eating up tons of bales, boxes, crates, sacks of flour and salt, hogsheads of molasses, salt pork, stoves, fish twine, freight of every description. The brawny, bronzed sailors at the bottom of the hold, who were catching the endless bales from the mighty crane-net-basket, resembled miniature men, as if I were seeing them from a plane flying high above the earth.

The *North Shore* looked like a satisfactory vessel for her job. In the years to follow I should come to love every solid plank of her, for I learned how faithfully she carried her important cargo through the roughest weather.

Gradually the disorder on the crowded deck resolved itself and precisely at four o'clock Captain Legault shouted, "All aboard! All hands on deck. Pull up the gangplank."

I was off on a new adventure, my objective the Grenfell Mission Station at Mutton Bay, hundreds of miles down the St. Lawrence River.

As we pulled away from the city there was so much of interest to be seen that a group of us went from side to side of the steamer watching the lovely Quebec landscape unroll before us. Those who had passed this way before were able to name some of the villages nestling close to the shore, each with its church spire pointing heavenward.

The time spent in the dining saloon seemed long to me—although I enjoyed my meal—for I did not want to miss a minute on deck. I shall never forget the beauty of the sunset on our first evening out.

The sun disappeared behind the hills more quickly and earlier than we are accustomed to in the central and southern part of Canada. At first I was disappointed, for I had heard of the beauty of the St. Lawrence River sunsets. But my disappointment did not last. The blue of the hills deepened into purple and then into darkness and then their lovely contours were etched against a blaze of glorious color, golden at first and finally a lovely rose.

The afterglow lasted a long time, and although the breeze was stiffening and growing colder, I watched until the last of the exquisite shades paled into misty grey and the hills lost their sharpness of outline and seemed almost menacing in their blackness and bulk.

Next morning came the first of our many stops to deliver freight. My roommate, Miss Wells, and I were on deck early sniffing the salty, fresh air when suddenly our foghorn boomed across the water. The captain shouted, "Heave to! Throw the anchors!" I rushed to see what was being "heaved to." There was not a building in sight and I never learned the name of our first stop. A rusty, rickety Tin Lizzie wheezed over a corduroy road and rattled to a standstill on the wobbly wharf. Our vessel swayed sideways, righted itself, the propeller gave one last churn, and we docked at the wharf.

Wearing wide-topped, hip-length, black rubber boots, which flapped like wings at every step, men swarmed about Lizzie. The first man spat generously on his hands, rubbed them together, and spoke to the next man, who repeated a similar spittle lubrication. They braced their feet, grunted, shoved, heaved to, then eased a monstrous puncheon—a mammoth, center-bulging barrel—to the ground. Two other men stepped forward and with a final push and heave the barrel rolled to the water's edge. We began to speculate what this puncheon might contain but we did not have long to wait.

The *North Shore* had scarcely bumped the wharf when Captain Legault shouted, "Throw her!" Straight as a lariat, one of the sailors flung a rope, which a shoreman caught skillfully. He ran with it and commenced to wind it round and round a large iron hook, driven deep into the pier.

Like magic, small boats were arriving seemingly from nowhere. There were motorboats, dinkies, and small hand-rowed boats called "kinoos." Each one brought one or two fat puncheons.

"How many quintals?" shouted the purser.

I had read about puncheons. Now, unless I wished to be dubbed a greenhorn, I must call a puncheon a quintal.

These quintals were full of fish, salted and packed for market.

The falconlike, iron crane creaked and groaned up from the hatch. Slowly it swung out over the deck rail. Then down, down, with its precious cargo to the waiting boats.

"Dunk her!" roared the engineer.

One of the fishermen jumped forward and unsnapped the hook. Boxes, cartons, and sacks spilled into the bobbing boats. Fishermen, swaying with the motion, quickly stowed the freight into mysterious corners of their boats.

Up and down went the basket-crane, scooping up quintals of fish from the shore and depositing bales of butter, beds, lumber, stoves, and washing machines in the boats. Lizzie, filled till she bulged aft and stern, bumped off home again. Somehow, sometime, she would reach it intact. With Lizzie went our last sight of a car for many months.

The screech and groan of the anchors being drawn up followed by the booming of the foghorn made the small motorboats and kinoos scatter like frightened chickens. The chug of motorboats died away in the distance as we swung out of the harbor.

At shelter Bay, headquarters of the famous Imperial Pulp Company, we made our next stop.

"We will be here until late tonight. Last chance to stretch your land legs," announced the captain.

As we filed down the gangplank we saw high above our heads two V-shaped boards formed into something like an eave trough. This, we learned, is called a sluice. Running water poured down its length, carrying along an endless procession of logs. As they reached the end of the sluice, one after another wavered in the air, then shot, straight as an arrow, down to the waiting men. Broad-shouldered, mahogany-skinned lumbermen snatched the logs and piled them in long tiers in the pit of the *S.S. Newcastle*—cordwood for Scotland.

Twelve feet up in the air, a six-inch plank walk ran along beside the sluice. This was the only connection between our vessel and the shore. Scared and shaking, high above the roaring water, we clung to a narrow rail. I kept one eye on the heavens and the other on the inferno below and managed to reach the shore.

The main attraction of the village was the lumbermen's messrooms. At the top of the steep bank the cook grinned at us. "Like to see our cookhouse?" he called. On a stick dangled four codfish, fresh from the water—tomorrow's luxurious dinner. In the messroom there were tables on both sides of the room surrounded by benches and set with thick earthen mugs, tin plates, soup bowls, and huge knives, forks, and spoons placed twelve inches apart. It was hard to imagine those broad-shouldered lumbermen wedging themselves into such cramped space.

A young lad, perhaps eighteen or nineteen years of age, who had obviously been helping the cook, was listening eagerly to all that was said. He looked as if he might be homesick and lonely and we said as much to the cook after he took us to the cookhouse and we had admired the row of delectable pies ready for supper.

"Could be. Son of a millionaire partner. Couldn't resist the night life of the big city so his dad shipped him up here. 'No favoritism, treat him like everybody else' were the orders. He's getting to be a first-class potato peeler and you outa hear him play the mouth organ evenings. It's a fair treat."

We wished that we could stay to hear him and encourage him by adding our applause to that of the men, but a blast from the *North Shore* warned us to make haste.

Our next stop was Clarke City, which is built several miles from the wharf and reached by a small jitney over rails. As the last drum of oil banged to the wharf, agonizing groans rose from the hold and commotion reigned below. A sailor had missed his footing and crashed down into the hold. The crane-basket hoisted him ashore and he was rushed to Clarke City to a doctor. A subdued hush settled over the sailors who had worked shoulder to shoulder with him. Later, we learned that he never returned to the ship.

From Clarke City we went across to Seven Isles, an Indian reservation. Solemn-looking Indians surrounded the steamer. While the freight was unloaded, we went ashore to see the sights. The swarthy Indian janitor of the tiny church proudly unlocked the door for us and by signs and broken English words explained the points of interest about the church and cemetery. His wife followed a few steps behind her husband with a bright-eyed little girl who eagerly grasped the coins we gave her, curtsied, and lisped, "Tank yous."

After we left Seven Isles the scenery changed. Gulls by hundreds circled above us. There were practically no trees, and barren, black, scraggy rocks and hills loomed on both sides of the river. This lack of trees, the number of gulls, and the immense, perpendicular rocks told us that we were leaving the beautiful St. Lawrence River and nearing the rough gulf water.

Night closed in and a thick fog enveloped us; heavy raindrops splashed out of the fog blanket. The air became chilly. So dense was the fog that Captain Legault ordered the sailors to drop anchor and "wait for weather." Since waiting for weather was no new experience for the crew, they were prepared to keep things lively. A photographer, on his way to the unveiling of the Greenley Island monument, got out his camera. Amid gales of laughter and singing, his mock photography and interview of a Very Important Person dispelled all thoughts of fog and danger.

At three o'clock in the morning the fog lifted and we steamed ahead. Sunday morning we entered Natashquan harbor where a Sabbath stillness shrouded everything. An old, weather-worn fisherman, slouched over the seat of a homemade, two-wheel dump cart, seemed part of the somnolent landscape, but a blast from our foghorn ended his snooze.

We could see Natashquan, the headquarters of the Hudson's Bay Post, in the distance. Our chief engineer, out for adventure, borrowed the one-horse shay. Miss Wells, a tourist, and I ran down the gangplank and begged to share his adventure. Legs dangling behind, we sat flat on the floor of that springless, cushionless cart and bumped through black muck and over corduroy logs two miles to the Post. When we arrived we realized that it really was the Sabbath here. The store was closed. The engineer spat his chagrin and muttered, "My bacca! What'll I chew?"

Back at the steamer, we found that to walk or stand was tolerable but to sit was impossible, so we crawled into bed and suffered in silence. Soon even seat bruises were minor thoughts as a typical Gulf night enveloped us.

All night long, the slush, slop, and slap of the waves pounded against the sides of the steamer. Briny spray came through the porthole ventilator into the upper berth. As the vessel rolled, lurched, and swayed, one by one we collapsed, reached out, and drew our seasick cups to our green-grey lips. Retching, tossing, and moaning we spent the night. Morning brought no relief. From Natashquan eastward both day and night seemed a horrible nightmare of briny odor and relentless sea.

But when the Grenfell Mission Hospital at Harrington Harbour loomed through the darkness like an oasis in a desert, our spirits revived. At three o'clock in the morning we cast anchor. Two passengers were to go ashore so we got up and dressed, after a fashion, uttering a prayer of thankfulness that we had survived the night.

Scarcely had we cast anchor at the wharf when a tall, bronzed young man, dressed in oilskins, sou'wester, and hip boots, came aboard. He was the Presbyterian student minister come to meet his sister. He went below for her trunk, shouldered it as if it were a feather, and strode up the stairs.

Another man, similarly dressed, stuck his head through the door and queried, "Are you the nurse for Mutton Bay?"

It was the doctor, so rather meekly I replied, "Yes."

Above the noise of the crane he shouted, "Sister Martin will come aboard to meet you."

It was a relief to know I would be met. I had spent many hours wondering how I would recognize Mutton Bay should we reach it in the night. Once I ventured to ask the engineer, "How shall I know Mutton Bay?"

"Don't worry, Sister," he chuckled, "you will know it. The first thing you see as we go around the point is the cemetery." This was not the most reassuring reply, but I was glad there was a cemetery because my relatives had predicted that I had only a fifty-fifty chance of returning alive from the Coast.

We did not stop long at Harrington Harbour. When daylight broke through the fog I peered out the porthole. We were threading our way around and among windswept rocks which looked as though some powerful, furious monster had riven them from top to bottom. Yawning chasms—relics of the ice period—divided the rocks so that one could walk hundreds of feet between them and see nothing but jagged, perpendicular walls.

Captain Legault made his way carefully among the treacherous shoals. Suddenly he bellowed, "Throw the anchors." Our foghorn echoed across the water as I rushed to the deck rail, eager for my first glimpse of Mutton Bay.

The engineer had been right. Mutton Bay nestled peacefully on the black rocks with the cemetery at one side in the foreground.

The fog had lifted and the sun was shining on the little village. I dragged my suitcases to the railing and gazed eagerly shoreward. I expected Sister Martin any moment, but as it happened she was detained and I had a quarter of an hour to get my bearings and survey the beauty spread out before me.

Within the two headlands that formed the sides of the cove were smaller projecting arms of land protecting smaller coves. And as if growing there, the weather-beaten wooden platforms, called stages, were part of the shore. At the top of each stage were compact, square, wooden, grey-green and brown houses; blue, green, brown, red, and grey roofs blended into the brown shale rock foundations. Scantily clothed barefoot boys hopped about as they pushed and guided toy sail boats through the shallow cove water away from imaginary, treacherous shoals which waited to wreck their vessels.

The serenity of the scene was disrupted by a bloodcurdling warning from our steamer. Men wearing flippety-floppy hip boots, their knees bent slightly forward and sideways to keep them from slipping on the uneven rocks, picked their way down to their stages. There they swung one foot, then the other, over the edge; rung by rung, hand over hand, they backed down the ladders. A carefully planned leap landed them safely in their swaying boats. With a whir of the motor the propellers churned the water and the boats headed toward the *North Shore.*

Higher up on the rocks, the mossy grass knolls were dotted with tethered wolf dogs. Straining to be free, with ears pricked forward and upward, they alone were restless. All else seemed peaceful and contented.

The spire of the new church in the making (replica of the old one) silhouetted against the horizon and sky was a magnet of welcome. I could imagine the bell softly ringing at the service hours and the worshippers slowly wending their way along the narrow, well-beaten paths which led from all directions to the church.

A few hundred feet eastward I could see the Grenfell Mission Station with its green roof and red walls standing firmly on a rock foundation. This was to be the scene of my future labors.

High above the roof of the Station, the sun glittered on a

lovely waterfall. From melting ice far above, the water came trickling through a narrow crevice down the rocks, then splashed into a pond at the bottom with a fine showing of misty spray. Hemmed in on three sides by cliffs, fed by the waterfall, fringed with green, leafy shrubs and furze, this pond gently rippled with the breeze. A mossy carpet sprinkled with pink blossoms and bright green leaves led up to the pond. Even from a distance, I could picture a fairy flitting lightly over this mossy carpet to the pond (later, knee-deep, squish-squashing in water-soaked shoes, deep in this moss, I did not think of fairies).

On the rocks near the dock I could see the wildflowers clearly. They were blooming profusely, making the most of the short northern summer. Through the velvety green and brown moss that carpeted the rocks, lambs'-quarters with tiny black eyes set in babyish faces, purple iris, and a bright orange flower I could not name thrust their short sturdy stems.

Behind the natural rock garden the great cliffs extended upward. Here was a little stunted shrubbery and beyond, the welcome spires of firs and spruces.

My eyes came back to the church and the Mission Station and the comfortable-looking homes. They were there because Dr. Wilfred Grenfell had visited the cove and had seen the needs of the people. I was proud to have the privilege of living and working here, of becoming part of the community life. I prayed to God that I, like Dr. Grenfell, might not fail His needy people.

These Coast people, I soon found, have a deep-rooted faith in the words "Grenfell" and "Grenfell Mission."

It was August 4, 1892, that Wilfred Grenfell, a young English doctor, landed in Labrador. He was so impressed by these God-fearing fisherfolk—materially poor yet spiritually kind, generous, and friendly—that he decided to devote his life to a "mission of mercy" among them. They were, he found, a people whose word was as good as a bond and he was won by their primitiveness, sincerity, and honesty.

For nearly fifty years Dr. Grenfell dedicated his life to the needs of his people in Newfoundland and Canadian Labrador. As he worked among them, healing their sick, guiding them in religious life, and encouraging them in their daily tasks, he realized the necessity of obliterating their illiteracy and ignorance. Though wind, waves, and barren rocks were more practical teachers than book education in fitting these people for their work, he felt a certain amount of book education would be like adding icing to a cake or leaven to bread.

In a short time the fisherfolk began to appreciate and love Dr. Grenfell. They welcomed him into their homes and into their hearts. To them he was like Him who came to those beside the Sea of Galilee bringing relief and blessing to body and soul.

Friends in England, the United States, and Canada rallied to Dr. Grenfell's appeal for financial support. From the most easterly to the extreme westerly parts of the Coast of Canadian Labrador the word "Grenfell" brought hope to isolated settlers in scattered hamlets.

Children fell over one another as they scrambled over the rocks, each hoping to be the first to announce, " 'T is Dr. Grenfell's boat be coming in," or "Dr. Grenfell's dog-team be coming down the hill."

Mothers brought out their best dishes and saw that the teakettle was boiling. " 'T is a wonderful cold trip," they exclaimed. "He'll be needing a hot cup of tea."

On the fishing stages rough fishermen would mutter, "Watch

your manners and your language. Dr. Grenfell be a Christian."

It was through his influence that doctors and nurses and voluntary social workers came to Labrador and that dentists travelled the Coast to relieve painful suffering. Later, through the Grenfell Hospitals and Outposts, industrial workers provided remunerative work for the women during the long shut-in winter days and evenings and new and secondhand clothing was made available to supplement scanty wardrobes.

The far-reaching influence of Dr. Grenfell still affects the whole life of patients and maids in training in the Outposts and hospitals in Canadian Labrador. They, in turn, carry this Christian atmosphere into their homes and community life in the scattered villages all along the bleak Coast. The inspired influence of the great Sir Wilfred Grenfell makes his name revered and recalls fond memories in the hearts of the fisherfolk.

WHILE I stood waiting for Sister Martin, all shapes and sizes of boats had been putting out from the shore. Like barnacles they clustered and clung to the boat and the swinging passenger ladder. In a few moments the deck swarmed with excited human beings shouting questions.

"Wats doing outside?"

"Did yous strike ice?"

"Yous wants some furs?"

"Any chocolate bars?"

"Candy, eh?"

"Yous all buying fish this year?"

"Good catch up West?"

In quick succession, the fishermen fired these questions as they strode along behind the purser. Placidly, he went on with his work, answering questions at the same time. When the purser became too busy, one of the mates gave the answers.

"Throw the rope."

"Yep, prices have gone up."

"Aft boy, aft, with that rope!"

"Furs, no, not so good this year."

"Bring her nearer!"

"Quick, throw her."

"Yep, ice all gone."

"Lower the ladder."

Excitement reigned. Sailors threw ropes, chains clanked, the crane creaked and groaned while freight was thrown and piled in a heap. I stood quietly beside my baggage, but as minutes passed I began to scan every new arrival anxiously for one that might resemble a nurse. Men and boys, in rubber trousers and hip boots, dodged everywhere, but there was not a skirt among them. I began to wonder if Sister Martin had forgotten that I was to arrive on this boat.

I had noticed an outstanding man come aboard, now he gave orders, asked questions, and directed the loading of the small boats. Tall, broad-shouldered, and thickset, with iron-grey hair and a moustache carefully curled upward at both ends, he displayed an air of dignified capability with every move. His orders were clear-cut and direct. Men jumped instantly to obey his commands. Captain Legault greeted him as an equal and he responded with respect but without inferior shyness. I was positive that he, like the towering church and Station, must play an important part in the life of Mutton Bay.

The men on board the *North Shore* called him "Uncle John" and it was this Uncle John who took time to say to me, "You must be the new Sister. Ise guess that'll be Sister Martin now."

He pointed to the shore where I saw a motorboat being pushed off with three people in it. As they came close to the steamer I could see grey hair escaping from beneath one sou'-wester and decided this must be Sister Martin. Agile as a fisherman, she stood upright in the bobbing boat, then scrambled up the swing ladder. Close behind her came another woman.

"I guess you are the new nurse we are expecting," said Sister Martin. "Sorry we were delayed, but you know, one of those last-minute patients." She introduced me to her companion, Sister Foster, a nurse from Harrington who was visiting at Mutton Bay. Then, in the same breath, she continued, "Any tourists aboard?"

Tourists seemed extremely important. Later, I discovered why.

The steamer remained in harbor only long enough to unload freight. To reach the Mutton Bay Station one had to go by boat. Voluntary contributions supported the Station. The more tourists shown about, the wider the publicity and therefore the greater the contributions.

I was no coward, neither did I wish to disgrace the nursing profession, but it was with a sinking heart that finally I walked to the swinging ladder, raised my eyes heavenward, and started to back down it. Wobbling, lurching, I was grabbed by two fishermen and swung from the bottom rung into the rocking boat. The engine sputtered, the propeller churned the water, and we chugged shoreward.

With a thud, our boat collided with a little wharf. Another ladder to climb and there at the top of the stage Uncle John was waiting to welcome me. He stretched down his huge, weather-worn hand and exclaimed, "Fish make the stage ladder wonderful slippery. Ise'll swing yous up." He tugged from above as I crawled up the slippery ladder. When I reached the top Uncle John commanded, "Heave to!"

And up I went over the top to the wooden stage. From there I slipped and sprawled over green, slimy rocks, waded in spongy, water-soaked moss, then hobbled down a corduroy bridge, made of uneven, small peeled poles, to the Station.

When I arrived Sister Martin was already propelling enthusiastic tourists from room to room.

"How lovely!" they gushed.

"What a grand piece of work!"

"How lonely you must be!"

"I must remember the Mission!"

As I tagged along behind Sister I am afraid I was not as enthusiastic as the tourists. At every step my vertebrae seemed to bounce against my stomach. I had been seasick and had kept down no food for two days. When the steamer whistle called Uncle John and the tourists back to the *North Shore*, I thought, surely *now* we'll eat. Once more I learned that on the Coast first things were placed first, and eating was considered to be of secondary importance.

Sister Martin and her guest went to the post office at the top of the rocks a few hundred feet from the shed, and since I had been shown my room, I decided to unpack. It seemed a long time before they returned with an armful of letters and parcels. They eagerly ripped open the letters, which they read and re-read. I had no idea then of the importance of mail which arrives so seldom; lonely, homesick, hungry, and weak, I felt insignificant and unwanted. Eventually, at six o'clock, Sister Martin decided it was time to eat. My stomach had long since reached the past-caring stage but after a hot dinner I felt refreshed. Now I wanted nothing so much in the world as rest and sleep.

How soon could I go to bed? As I asked myself the question Uncle John came around the rocks with a load of supplies! Men scrambled up the cliff with bales and boxes on their shoulders. Back and forth they went, and higher grew the piles on the floor. Sleep had to be forgotten while the three of us checked, rechecked, opened, and packed away drugs and supplies into every available corner.

By nine o'clock my head was in a whirl, my legs were like lead, and my body reeked with woollen odors. Now, I decided, I can drag off my woollens, take a bath, and get to sleep. But with the last bale came a man holding a handkerchief tightly against the palm of his left hand. Blood oozed between his fingers and left red splotches on kitchen and hall floors. Sister Martin put a kidney basin under the dripping hand, opened her emergency kit, swabbed on green soap and alcohol, then set to work. With each pull of the sutures through that tough palm a cold shiver coursed up and down my spine. Feeling smaller, weaker, and even shakier than I had as a probationer, I watched and wondered what would happen when I was alone.

Sunday morning I said good-bye to Sisters Martin and Foster and watched the steamer disappear around the rocks. I felt very much alone.

Suddenly Annie, Sister Martin's maid, sobbed. "Hern's gone! What'll wes do when wes gets sick? Hern knew just what to do for everything." She mopped her apron across her eyes as two big tears splashed on her white blouse. Then she added, "Ise forgets yous is here. Wese better go back and do the dishes or wes'll be late for service."

I came back to earth and recalled that it was my first Sunday in Mutton Bay.

Since a new Anglican church was being erected, services were held in a small, dilapidated village schoolhouse. "In order to get a bench, usn always goes as soon as the first bell finishes ringing," Annie informed me.

In other words, half an hour before service was to start.

We thought we heard the first bell ring, so leisurely we strolled over to the church. As we entered the vestry Annie gasped and whispered, "It musta been the last bell. Service is half over."

With all eyes on me, I had to march to the second seat from the front and sit down. Not being an Anglican, I opened the prayer book at random and pretended to follow the service with my lips. The clergyman, Mr. Moak, stopped the service, called his young son up to him and passed him an open prayer book with whispered instructions. His hobnailed boots made a great noise in the stillness as the lad came clumping down the aisle and handed it to me. I accepted the book. The boy went back to his seat and the service continued.

During the chanting which followed I had time to glance about. A wide blackboard, covered with large, round, colored child's letters, was the altar background. Children's drawings were pasted at irregular intervals on the walls; behind Mr. Moak was a small disreputable-looking organ, minus some of its keys. Yet, in that quaint schoolhouse-church, the reverence and quietness was greater than it is in many huge cathedrals.

Outside, the waves gently lapped the rocks and children's happy voices harmonized with the solemn Sabbath stillness.

Lack of an organist did not prevent our praising the Lord. Loud, vibrating, thankful hallelujahs ascended. As the last notes rolled skyward Mr. Moak said, "Let us pray." Humbly I knelt, but more humiliation awaited me. The kneeling bench shot out from my, by now, extremely humble knees. With a quick, noiseless scramble I dragged the bench back under my knees. While good Christian souls all about me were earnestly praying with bowed heads, I longed to disappear out the door. After the prayer I listened to what seemed the longest sermon I ever had heard and then had to face the congregation for my first formal introduction.

Not very much was said, for the people here are apt to be taciturn with strangers, but their hands clasped mine in a firm friendly fashion and my little humiliations and loneliness were quickly forgotten.

August is one of the finest months in this part of Labrador. This Sunday afternoon was exceptionally pleasant, so old and young strolled up the hills. Like seals they stretched and basked in the sun while the children frisked about like lambs. Annie and I took a walk over the rocks then squashed across the soggy moss. A good Christian does not pick berries on the Sabbath in Mutton Bay, but since I had never tasted a bagh (or bake) apple, I am certain the good Lord understood my temptation, when Annie's back was turned, to pop one into my mouth. This Labrador berry has a delicious flavor not tasted elsewhere; in the yellow stage just before it turns ripe it resembles a raspberry. When it is ripe it stands upright, one berry to a stem, instead of hanging down. Many of these berries are eaten as fast as they ripen, yet there always seems to be a supply for winter use.

Arms of the Gulf flow far in between land points. These fingers of water are called "tickles." The pond among the rocks which I had seen from the *North Shore* emptied into one of these tickles. In summer, Annie told me, boats row across the tickle and catch barrels of water at the mouth of the pond's overflow; in winter dogs are hitched to sleds, called komatics, barrels roped on to the slats of the komatic, holes are cut in the ice, and the precious water dipped up.

Today a faint ripple stirred the crystal clear surface of the pond. Water wigglers and bugs chased each other on the muddy surface near us, while lily pads, with pink-white blossoms, floated on the opposite side.

The wilderness was all about us and everywhere was beauty and quietness. When the sun sank below the horizon, the air grew chilly and crept into our bones and we hastened back to the Station.

New and strenuous duties were ahead of me, and I would need moral and spiritual strength to carry me through the coming week, so as soon as the first church bell ceased ringing for evening service, we made certain to be there for an early bench.

Coast Anglican services are prolonged to the limit; we listened to another long sermon and liked it. After the benediction we stepped outside into the fragrant darkness, and more introductions were made and friendly hands clasped mine.

My first Sunday in Mutton Bay was over—or so I thought—and I felt refreshed and heartened.

When I drew near the Station I could see two persons slowly and laboriously climbing over the edge of their kinoo, which was tied at our rocks. I could not mistake the implications of that ponderous figure and my heart missed a beat. So soon, I must face this task alone, with no doctor to advise or nurse to help, a stranger among strange people with strange customs.

By the time I arrived at the kitchen door a man and woman stood waiting patiently. Mrs. Brown explained, "My time is tomorrow, so my man brought me up. He has to go home to the children."

She had come fifteen miles in a kinoo, confident that Sister would see her through "her time." I, less confident, took her to the ward. My consternation heightened as she continued, "When my first baby was coming Ise had one convulsion after another and then a dead baby." This information did not help and I lay down on my bed fully clothed, ready for action, and determined not to fall asleep.

At midnight, as if in a dream I heard, "Sister, Sister, are yous awake?" At first I could not recall where I was or who wanted me. Suddenly I remembered and ran across the hall to Mrs. Brown's ward.

Her pains grew harder and longer; it seemed as though morning would never come. The knowledge that the telegraph office would be open at eight o'clock gave me some comfort; but Sister Martin had told me the doctor did not encourage calls for minor troubles, that it was permissible to call for advice only in extremely severe cases. Over and over I asked myself if this was indeed an extremely severe case. Should I take a chance? Would the doctor reprimand me if anything went wrong?

Would he lose confidence in me if I could not tackle a simple maternity case alone?

While I tried to come to a decision night slipped into day. Day always strengthens confidence, so I decided to go ahead alone and Providence helped me over the nerve-racking period of waiting. Annie went ahead with her Monday morning's wash and I put a cake in the oven to bake.

As I closed the oven, Uncle John stuck his head through the kitchen door, announced, "Tourists," and disappeared. For some reason we had not heard the *North Shore* enter the harbor, en route to Quebec.

This time I, as hostess, piloted those enthusiastic, inquisitive tourists from attic to kitchen. As they departed, Mrs. Brown shouted downstairs, "Herns getting near." There was no time to reconsider my decision; action was needed immediately. Half an hour later a fine ten-pound girl arrived. Downstairs Annie shouted, "Yous cake, she's in cinders. Yous never said for mes to take hern out."

Such a minor catastrophe as a burned cake did not trouble me. I could deliver a baby. The Lord willing, everything would be all right. A weight rolled off my shoulders. I carried a rocking chair out to our little porch and gazed over the peaceful water, and I too became calm. The barking of dogs seemed more friendly. Children's laughter was more merry. The waves had a more homey sound as they lapped the rocks. The putt of motor-boats, carried by the soft sea breeze, was more gently familiar. All these sounds seemed to be whispering, "You are part of us."

The twilight deepened and tired fishermen, who had been jigging for squid for the next day's bait, whistled and sang as they guided their boats to the home wharves. Then darkness

enveloped the village. It was a joy to be alive and to have a part to play in the little community. City hubbub, smoke, noise, greed, and grimy coal-dust-laden air were a million miles away. Relaxed and invigorated, my mind at peace, I went inside.

Next day I frantically went through my medical books to discover what I could about anaemia, for Mrs. Brown had informed me she was anaemic. The authors of my medical books told me that anaemic patients should have lots of cow's milk and cereal, especially if they are nursing babies. Cows give milk, but not on the Coast, because there are no cows. Confident that I could cure Mrs. Brown I gave her evaporated milk to drink, evaporated milk on her cereal, evaporated milk in her tea and cocoa, and worked in extra servings at bedtime.

The third night, certain that I would discharge a non-anaemic patient, I enjoyed my first sound sleep since the baby was born. At six o'clock in the morning I was awakened with a whispered, "*Sister*." Then, more loudly, I heard, "Ise couldn't stand it any longer. My bed is flooded with milk."

The baby was having her early morning breakfast. From flood appearance she should have been quadruplets. Milk, like a geyser, sprayed from Mrs. Brown's breasts; I plumped on the breast pump and set to work. Persistently baby and I pumped and pulled and soon, for the time being, the situation was under control. The baby let go and, at last, rolled off to sleep. I stood holding a huge glass of human milk. Annie was in the kitchen when I went down to throw the milk into the sink. As soon as she saw my extravagance she shouted, "Sister, don't waste it. Give it to the puppy." She took the glass outside and soon returned followed by a bulging puppy, licking his milky chops.

Nothing must be wasted on the Coast. There is a use for every-

thing. For three days pup and babe shared the milk feasts while I fed Mrs. Brown dry food and walked with less confident tread. When I discovered that Mrs. Brown had Eskimo blood in her veins I surmised that Eskimos are not milk drinkers and resolved that my next anaemic patient would be fed on seal meat or fish.

Ten days later a happy father lifted a well mother and a contented baby into his kinoo. As they rowed away I bade them Godspeed, faced the Station once more, and wondered what my next adventure would be.

DURING my first weeks in Mutton Bay, I was impressed by the extreme taciturnity of the people; when they have nothing to communicate they say nothing! The men especially may sit for hours and not speak a word. At first this silence seemed strained and hard to endure with equanimity. But soon I realized that it was more friendly than talk about our neighbors or the minister's wife. I learned to sit calmly and silently in some home during a raging storm while waiting for the advent of a new baby or the crisis of a pneumonia patient. During these silent sittings I realized how unnecessary, and how often harmful and ruthless, was our daily, social city conversation. But I did long at times for someone with whom I might exchange a few words about something besides fish, boats, weather, price of seal, lead dogs, traps, and mail.

Yet what could be more vitally interesting to these fishermen—and to their wives and children? The whim of the sea may mean no seal, few fish, therefore no boots, no clothing or food for the family. Loss of a lead dog may mean no wood for winter; loss of a trap may mean no fresh winter meat.

Their whole livelihood depends on The Big Four—codfish, herring, lobster, and salmon. (On the Coast "fish" always means codfish. Other species are called by different names.) In the late fall and early spring seal fishing is carried on by some of the men, and in deep winter many go inland trapping.

Many of the fishermen depend on sail and rowboats but they cannot support a family without help from relatives or the Mission unless they have better equipment. The successful progressive fisherman needs nets, bobbers, trawls, quintals, salt, traps, a motorboat. Of course many of them do make a living without all of these.

The Coast fisherman works hard. His hours are long; except for the Sabbath, holidays are unknown to him as, day after day the same tasks, varying somewhat with the season, have to be done. Fish get into the nets and have to be removed on all holidays except the Sabbath. If the seal are running the men work on Christmas Day; if not, it is the one weekday of the year they do not work.

Poor financially, the fisherfolk possess that contentment within their homes and with their lot that philosophers say is the heart of happiness. Their struggle is with life; their joys are in their achievements in the constant struggle to keep themselves and families above the starvation mark.

Boys and girls age prematurely. Their early knowledge of the hardships of a fisherman's life, of suffering and sudden death, make them old before their time. By the time a boy is fifteen he has shared the awful silence of long winter nights; he has faced sudden, furious blizzards to bring help to travailing women or dying relatives; he has raced with death through floating ice, slob water, and treacherous currents. And through it all, he has reached a faith that Someone mightier than he is in charge. Yet he knows, at times, he must face a crisis first and pray afterward. When his dogs and komatic suddenly dangle over open water, he must decide on action or prayer or both. A quick, strong arm and a whip will send the dogs and himself to safety while a pause for prayer might be fatal.

In these little fishing villages friendliness and hospitality are more valuable than efficiency. The successful fisherman is efficiency personified, but the friendliness and co-operative spirit of all his neighbors make possible his efficiency. They pull together through blizzards, through rain torrents, through epidemics. They parcel out food until the steamer arrives. They "gang-up," using manpower for horsepower to rebuild and refloat boats. They have a "bee" and together knit the precious nets. They battle together through black fly seasons and bad fish catches. When stark necessity faces them, their strength and courage pull them through the worst times.

The fisherman's life is hard but it has none of the deadly monotony of the factory worker's. The hazards of the sea take care of that.

Another fine thing about the fisherman's life as I saw it was that the family worked together as a unit within the larger co-operation of the community. When the fish has been caught and brought home it has to be cleaned, perhaps salted, or dried, or smoked. Every member of the family does his share and the father, the head of the family, is his own boss; he is proprietor and employee and utilizer of his own products.

This sort of family industry brings contentment. It seems to work admirably.

Ever since my arrival in Mutton Bay I had eaten canned, fresh, salt, dried, and smoked fish; I had smelled it and slipped on it on the stages and of course I had heard much talk about it. But I had not yet seen fish caught in the nets and traps. Mr. Benny, when I told him of my ignorance, promised to take me the first time we could arrange it.

One morning I was swallowing the last mouthful of breakfast when Annie called, "Blanche, herns acomin runnin."

Blanche bounced in, dropped into the rocking chair and gasped, "Pa says if yous wants to go with hes fishing, wes going in ten minutes. Donnie and me wes going too."

Annie collected my rubber boat togs while I dragged on heavy woollens.

In ten minutes I was at the stage where Mr. Benny stood ready to push off. "Jump in!" he shouted. I obeyed and John, his fifteen-year-old son, steered the boat away from the wharf. Ted, eighteen years old and already a trusted fisherman, tended the engine.

Mr. Benny eased his sciatic limbs to a comfortable resting angle and pulled out his pipe. He leaned his head below the boat edge, cupped his hands about a match, and gave a few pulls. As curling clouds of smoke rose above his head, he settled down to entertain me with tales of his own heroic deeds and unsurpassed ability.

"Ise always learns my youngsters to be the bestest fishermen," he boasted. "That's why theyse always gets the mostest catches. Donnie, hims only four, but this morning Ise sez to hes 'tis time yous started to be a fisherman, out yous goes today.' Mines always obeys me. Donnie jumped into his overalls. There's John, Ise remembers when hims was Donnie's age. Ise took hims and Ise learned hes ever since. At fifteen hes can handle a boat better'n any boy in this village. Ted, hims a good un. The three of wes has the bestest outfit in this harbor. Today yous'll see our nets will be full. That's because Ise knows where to set our nets. Other men goes by chance, but Ise tells yous Ise knows how to fish."

He spat a brown streak over the edge of the boat and proudly swung his head from side to side as if to indicate that he was the best spitter as well as the best fisherman in all of Labrador.

John guided the boat past shoals into deep water, where it took the waves lightly as the land dwindled to a fine horizon line.

Donnie, like his father in miniature, swaggered up and down the boat balancing his rickety, deformed body to the rhythmic sway of the boat. His wrinkled, drawn skin, stretched tightly across his wan face, gave him the appearance of a little old man. Pot-bellied from lack of proper food, his abdomen seemed to extend to his bowed knees.

His sister, Blanche, had outgrown her homespun dress. The skirt ended halfway between her hips and knees. Three inches shorter than normal girls of her age and ten pounds underweight, she sat there and worshipped her father and brothers as they cheerfully whistled and chatted, guiding their boat among treacherous shoals seemingly without effort.

We rode buoyantly on the crest of the waves as water rolled heavily under the keel. There, lightly poised for a moment, we hung, then down we swooped, down the green foam-flecked slope into the trough of a giant wave. Our boat met the impact, cut the water, and righted itself. This was rough water indeed.

Both Donnie and Blanche were deathly seasick. Down went the boat and up came their breakfasts. They clung to the sides, not able to raise their heads. The sea, not their father, was "learning" them to be fishermen. I realized that the sea had to be conquered before a boy would make a fisherman, and I knew also that soft words and sympathy would never make a hardy, efficient fisherman. But my heart ached for those babies and I longed to offer a few comforting words. John poked Donnie in the ribs and snickered, "A great help yous'll be," and Mr. Benny jeered at him with, "What a fisherman yous will make!" as he turned to me with, "That's how Ise learns em." He seemed almost to enjoy their suffering. Donnie never whimpered or uttered a word as the swells and rolling increased; he seemed to take it as part of his life.

(Fourteen years later, I learned that Donnie, an excellent fisherman, went out alone and met a tragic death. His boat was seen floating so men went to investigate. He must have entangled his foot in the tow rope somehow and lost his foothold. His body was found with part of the rope on his foot.

The sea is a hard master; mistakes are not forgiven. Parents know this, and that is why they train their children, sometimes ruthlessly, to cope with the hard conditions of life on the Coast.)

We did not make a good haul that day, for sea and weather were against us. At least Mr. Benny was not satisfied; but when the net was raised and the contents spilled into the boat there seemed to me to be a great many slippery cod. Two fine salmon had also strayed into the cod net. The silver salmon are exquisitely beautiful fish, and when John held them up in the sunlight their silvery sheen, gasping gills, and bright black eyes made me feel like a murderer. I did not feel the same about the codfish. Its white flesh is the bread of life for the fisherman on that part of the Coast, its tongues provide him with a delicacy he enjoys, its livers are good for anaemic persons and provide the purest cod-liver oil.

One day I spent long hours in a village home waiting while a baby made up its mind to come into the world. The grandmother, Mrs. Black, and I knitted and talked while we sat by the fire during the intervals when we could do nothing for the patient. And to my delight our conversation was not about the weather, nor yet about fish. Education and religion were this fine old lady's topics.

Mrs. Black deplored the difficulties in the way of the children's schooling. She did not see how they all could be overcome, but did believe that some of the parents might be helped to realize how important it was that their children should have as good an education as possible. And how proud she was that her nine-year-old granddaughter could read what the papers and magazines said about the Outside!

Her great love was her church. She was a Protestant and longed for the day when they would have a resident clergyman.

Mutton Bay was an Anglican and Roman Catholic community

—the clergy of these two churches at this time had charge of all the souls along the Coast and called at Mutton Bay at more or less regular intervals. As a result, other denominational members, desiring the Gospel message, wishing their children to be baptized and to have some religious education, and needing someone to whom they might turn when death overtook them, had become Anglicans or Roman Catholics. In early days Moravian missionaries had left a deep and lasting influence on the lives of the people on the Coast and later this had kept the Gospel alive when no clergyman or priest was available.

Theoretically, every baby is born an Anglican or a Roman Catholic, but actually the decision is not made before birth and many times not by one or both parents. Since there is much intermarriage of members of these two churches the deciding factor is often uncertain until the last minute before baptism. All the parents were anxious to have their babies baptized as soon as possible and when one parent was Protestant and the other Roman Catholic, the baby entered this world with a twofold pull. One parent and grandparent prayed for a Protestant offspring. The other parent and grandparent prayed for a Catholic child. Frequently chance settled the question. If an Anglican clergyman came around the point before a Catholic priest, the baby was made a good Anglican, or vice versa if a Roman Catholic priest entered the harbor first.

Mrs. Black's daughter-in-law was a Catholic and when at four o'clock in the morning a strapping ten-pound boy thrust himself into this frigid atmosphere, I chuckled and wondered whether I had helped increase the Anglican flock or the Roman Catholic membership.

Daily I snowshoed over and cared for the Roman Catholic

mother in the home of the Protestant grandmother and the non-denominational baby. On the fifth day, like a clucking hen, the Protestant grandmother hovered over me as I bathed the baby. She twisted her apron and fidgeted from one foot to the other until I packed my bag and went out the door, then she whispered, "Mr. Moak came into the village this morning. Will yous loan us your christening gown, and will yous ask Mr. Moak to come right away and baptize the baby? Wese wants hes quick. Ise wants the baby to be a Protestant. They think the Catholic priest will be in the harbor this afternoon. Plez, plez, tell hes to come quick."

By the skin of his teeth, Mr. Moak and our christening robe made this boy an Anglican. Just four hours too late the Catholic priest arrived. The relatives are certain that it was God's will this baby should be a Protestant.

In Mutton Bay, to be religious, one must be an Anglican or a Roman Catholic. I was a commissioned missionary of another denomination and was allowed to teach in the Mutton Bay Anglican Sunday School, to lead the Girl Guides, help with the Women's Association, and stand as godmother for certain babies, but they did not consider it right that I should take communion or have any part in the intimate life of the church. Possessing certain signed documents from the bishop and working with a broad-minded clergyman, I might have been able to receive permission to take communion in the church; but I did not wish to press my desire, and I needed no permission from either Anglican or Catholic to have communion with God in my private life.

There can scarcely be a doubt that religion, sincere or not, plays a large part in the lives of most individuals and communities. Mutton Bay was no exception. Births, baptisms, deaths, and funerals, even if there were no desire for spiritual enlightenment and comfort, kept the people in close contact with the church.

As I visited in the homes—often in times of serious illness—I learned much about the religious faith of the people.

They desired to live according to the rules of their church, and also, since they had Bibles, as Christ had taught. The Sabbath was kept a holy day of rest. The older people believed that it was God's law that there should be no unnecessary work on the Sabbath. If they did unnecessary work they believed something tragic would happen to them or their families. The provincial law forbids fishing on Sunday. Enforced or voluntary, it is a day of rest, worship, and visiting for most of the intelligent fisherfolk.

I learned how closely traditional superstitions and religion are interwoven. If a person, especially a clergyman, is the latest newcomer in the village and the fishing catch is poor, he is known to be the "Jonah." On the other hand, if there is a bounteous catch, he is doubly welcome. A storm at sea, a dog howling, and certain screaming of gulls indicates someone has gone or will go to a watery grave. A baby born with a caul over its face is born lucky. This caul is given to a sea captain, who will carry it on his vessel. While carrying it his vessel will be lucky. Babies, even a few minutes or a few days old, must not die unbaptized or they will be lost forever. Work started on certain days or certain phases of the moon will be disastrous.

Justly or unjustly, there is a tendency to consider everything to be the result of God's will. Births, deaths, good catch, bad catch, famine, disease, good or bad weather, and rough seas are all God's will. Most of the people do not seem to realize that controllable calamities may arise from a tendency to laziness. Many unsatisfactory conditions could be changed with a little more individual exertion and ambition. Yet, so much of their living, day and night, winter and summer, depends on the sea and weather, that it is hard to draw a line between God's will and their shirked responsibility.

It was God's will that ten-year-old Sammy was taken. Never for a moment did his parents and their friends consider it man's responsibility that the germ which caused his death came from uncleanness in his home. Against his father's wishes, John went out to sea in a blinding blizzard and never came home. They told me it was God's will that he was drowned.

Education, of course, is closely associated with religion in shaping the lives of the Coast people. It is impossible to call them either literate or illiterate; there was a combination of both types. Many facts were appalling to an Off-coaster. In 1928, hundreds of children did not attend school beyond the fourth grade and many had never been in a classroom. Since most of their grandparents and many of their parents had never had an opportunity to attend school, it is not surprising that a grade seven pupil was considered very well educated.

A school education is hard for many of the people to achieve for their children. In some instances, the distance to the schoolhouse is short but it is necessary to cross water, ice, rocks, or snowbanks and this is dangerous for small children. Their fathers and older brothers are away fishing, sealing, or woodcutting from daylight to dark. Their mothers are shut in with the tiny tots so there is no one to row the children across, guide them safely among dogs, or see that they are not caught in a sudden blizzard and frozen to death.

From November to May, many families live in shanties far inland while cutting wood, and their children can not get to school during these months. The schools are closed for the summer. Other families move to lighthouses early in June and do not come inland again until December. These children have no schooling except for a few winter months.

Schoolhouses have to be heated, so instead of paying a school tax, every family who has a child or children attending school has to supply a cord of wood each term. If more is needed it is supplied by the fathers of the larger families. The men and older boys take turns lighting the fires. Occasionally an illiterate, bull-headed father decides he is not going to exert himself to haul wood for his children's education. If he does not provide wood his children cannot attend school and school has to close until someone else supplies fuel. If the person next in line has procrastinated, he may have to go back into the woods to cut wood and school may be closed for several days. When a Labrador blizzard strikes, it is unsafe for a child to venture outside for several days, so school automatically closes. Some years ago compulsory education became law in Quebec but no law compels a father to provide wood. Since Mutton Bay territory is unorganized and unpoliced, it is a law unto itself.

No city teacher can realize what these disruptions mean to classes. Under adverse conditions, in a few short months, these conscientious Labrador teachers produce almost miraculous results. It only takes a few days living here to realize what education means to the people. I walked through a fishing stage and noticed several series of XXX's cut into the wall. "What are these?" I enquired of Tom, an old fisherman. "Wal, yous sees, it's this way. Yous knows that the trading schooners used to come across from Halifax and down from Quebec. Theys brought usn molasses, lard, oatmeal, salt pork, and flour for our fish. Wes had to knows how many quintals of fish wes had to gives em in exchange. Wes never knew figgers so wes make an X on the wall every time wes fill a quintal with fish. The captain of the schooner counted the X's and told usn how many quintals and how much he'd pay for what he brought us. Wes knows theyse were doing us (exploiting) but what could wes do? Wes had to live. That's why Ise wants my boys to learn 'rithmetic. Now, my Johnny, hes can figger and hes knows the top price of food and fish. Eddication is mighty wonderful for this village."

An old, rheumatic, crippled grandmother eagerly scanned some magazine pictures which I had given her and said proudly, "Wait till our Suse comes home from school. Hern will read mes all about what it says. Hern knows everything. Hern can figger. Hern can read and hern even knows stories about England and Vancouver." To herself, she muttered, "Eddication sure is mighty wonderful. Wes never got it."

There is a dearth of teachers and leadership which can be given only by persons interested in the actual needs of individuals, by those who are willing to live in isolated districts, in homes where food consists of the bare necessities, and where plumbing conveniences and sanitation are unknown.

Many fisherfolk see no reason why their children need attend school regularly, therefore the teacher has to create an interest among the parents for something more than reading, writing, and figures. Schoolhouses are drab, dark, dusty, draughty, barn-like buildings with outside toilets. In the winter, if it were not for the Missions, many children would not have sufficiently warm clothing to attend school.

It would be simple foolishness, of course, to believe that all the education the children received was from a teacher in a schoolhouse. In every home the education of the children, although it does not proceed along formal lines, is a matter of great importance—for economic if for no other reasons. Boys learn the secrets of their calling from their fathers and at a very early age are able to help with tasks, such as net-mending, which can be done at home. And the little girls learn much from their mothers and are soon—too soon, I felt—grave and responsible.

Some parents want more than they or the village school can give their children. In practically every village there is someone who has caught the vision of a deeper life enjoyed by receiving more education and he or she is willing to undergo hardships and sacrifices to give the children better schooling. These are the people who promote progress and carry the burden of the village in order to raise the standard of living.

Uncle John was such a visionary man in Mutton Bay. He was thrifty, energetic, sympathetic, co-operative, and progressive; yet he could read but little and write less. His sons and daughter received an Off-coast education and then returned to help him carry on his business.

Uncle John was the prop, the support of the whole village. He had impressed me with his efficiency and kindness the day I landed in Mutton Bay and as long as I was there my respect for him deepened. When food was scarce he shared his own meager store with the less fortunate; when laziness caused want, his tongue did not spare the shirker but then John would offer him work in exchange for food. He would sit up all night with a dying neighbor doing all in his power to ease the pain. He had learned much through having people turn to him when in trouble. He did not confine his ministrations to Mutton Bay. An emergency call from one of the more isolated coves would take him out over an almost impassable sea. When death visited the village he was there to comfort the mourners. He came with saw and hammer to build the casket, and, if no clergyman was available, he would partly read, partly recite the burial service. A useful, upright member of our community and a fine Christian was Uncle John.

AUGUST weather is usually the best of the year and the Coast folk try to get all the enjoyment possible out of calmer seas and bright summer skies. Yet August is not without its own difficulties. It is the month of black flies and dysentery and that spells a busy time for the Mission Stations. It is the month of long fishing days and injured hands. For galled fingers, infected finger joints unknown except in fishing districts, are one of the dangerous and painful hazards of the fisherman's life.

As the boat bobs on the water, inch by inch the fisherman

plays off his line, which has hooks attached to the end of it. These capelin or herring baited hooks dangle just ahead of the fish and appear to be hastening to escape the fish's jaws. Finally, with a spurt, the fish leaps forward and gobbles the bait. Too late, it finds imbedded in the tempting bait one of those sharp-pointed, brad hooks which dig unmercifully into the walls of its mouth. A sudden jerk pulls the line taut and the struggle is on between fisherman and fish. This taut line saws back and forth through and over the two front finger joints. The line loses an inch, then gains a foot until with a final struggle the exhausted fish is flung over the edge of the boat. Day after day, this line saws across the fingers, cutting deeper and deeper. Each morning a new skin tissue starts to form, but by noon the skin is worn away and the old cut reopened. During this process of breaking down and building up, if the patient is in a weakened condition, infection sets in. By August this rut across the fingers at the second joints is nearly worn down to the bone.

No matter how raw or sore his fingers are, the fisherman must keep going. Fish mean his family's winter food. He sops up the blood, pays out the line, which cuts deeper sending fiery darts of pain up his arm. Flies loaded with vicious germs crawl into these sores and inflammation sets in, followed by green pus, and it is impossible for the man to go out fishing. He comes to the Station with galled fingers. Properly looked after, washed with antiseptic solution, soothed with ointment, these sores respond to treatment. If a man could stop work and let his fingers heal for a week, much suffering could be avoided; but a day lost may mean a month's food. There is no unemployment insurance, no workmen's compensation for him. He must work or starve. All I could hope to do was to prevent infections spreading throughout the body and to lessen the pain somewhat. A line passing over adhesive and bandage prevented contact with the sore but, by night, the white bandage had been soaked, dried, and re-soaked so many times with human and fish blood, salt water, and dirt, that it resembled a black stove cloth.

At the same time as the galled finger wounds are mosquito and black fly infections. Coast mosquitoes do not bite. They grab a chunk and run away to digest it! As they buzz about the head and neck they sound almost as loud as an aeroplane entering a landing field.

Like swarms of bees, small black flies buzz over exposed parts of the body and limbs. Labrador August, known as dog days, really should be fly days. In sultry scorching weather with no breeze, the black flies stick to faces, necks, arms, and legs. Fishermen beat the flies away and continue to rip out bloody fish entrails, then rub their necks with the backs of their hands; infected bites are the result. Tiny red-hot needles pierce the nerve endings as the flies tenaciously cling, like leeches, and suck the human blood.

Daily, two or three patients came with infected areas on their necks. The wretched flies had opened the skin and germs had penetrated deep into flesh and muscles. Huge reddened areas, swollen and painful, with deep-seated pus pockets, required soakings and scalpel incisions. When the sharp point of the scalpel pricked the infected spots, thick, green pus spurted up and ran down the patient's neck into a waiting basin. The infected bites had a tough, stringy, boillike core deeply imbedded in the flesh, which emitted a putrid odor. If the men came regularly the angry sores cleared sufficiently for me to lift out the pus-laden core with a pair of forceps. Then an alcohol-saturated cotton plug, in contact with sun and salt water, did the rest. However, a life-long scar remained. Many never came regularly, thus weeks of treatment were necessary.

Tired and weak from infections, the men were easy prey later in the year for bacterial germs: colds, dysentery, and other diseases.

Besides mosquitoes and black fly infections, August on the Coast is baby and dysentery month. The first ripe berry is the bagh apple. When it is ripening it resembles the raspberry, as I earlier noted, or a tiny Gravenstein apple. In a few days it becomes a lovely soft and dull yellow-orange color which tempts young and old. Youngsters, unable to wait, snatch handfuls of these sour berries which they crunch and swallow half-chewed. By night a rebelling tummy brings the nurse and castor oil. Before the bagh apple has run its course, green blueberries, spice berries, and moss blackberries make it necessary to continue the castor oil.

Before the blueberries are finished the famous Coast redberries, clinging to the mossy, rocky slopes, begin to ripen. Picking these berries necessitates much stooping and bending which brings different problems. Expectant mothers climb from rock to moss, stoop, squat, crawl, and stretch their arms for berries. Tired and stiff they trudge home carrying heavy pails of berries, dragging one or more tired, peevish youngsters. Almost exhausted, the mother prepares supper for her hungry brood. About midnight a shout comes upstairs, "Sister, a baby case." The nurse grabs the ever-ready, sterile maternity kit, and another fisherman is added to the already overflowing household.

Dressing galled fingers and fly bites, holding noses for castor oil to roll down tummies full of green berries or polluted water, "borning" new arrivals, sterilizing kits, giving aspirins, and canning berries made August slip away before I realized it.

On the afternoon of the thirtieth at three o'clock, two expectant mothers trudged past the Station, each dragging two sagging youngsters. It was unusual for berry pickers to return so early in the afternoon so I went out on the porch and glanced at the sky. A ponderous, black cloud was rolling in from the east. The dogs and birds were uneasy and excited. Periodically, a dog would point his nose skyward and utter a long-drawn-out wolf howl. At this signal every dog in the harbor joined in and the chorus echoed across the water.

Shrieking as they flew, gulls dived and hovered over the water.

An uncanny instinct drove the youngsters closer to the rocky shores with their play boats.

The sky grew darker, the wind wailed louder, and an unearthly calm settled over the whole harbor. By four o'clock the screaming gulls, howling dogs, and the tense air grew almost unbearable. Everything cried danger.

I had heard that phenomenal tidal waves had carried away whole villages, that earthquakes had been foretold, that Jehovah's Witnesses were predicting the end of the world, and I had not been shaken. This first time I experienced the approach of a Labrador storm, I may as well confess I felt frightened and awed. I went upstairs, pinned my money in a handkerchief and placed it inside my uniform pocket. My uniform and money would go with me. There was nothing to do but wait.

Electrically-charged air made it impossible to settle to routine work. I missed Annie, who was away for the day. Every noise echoed through the empty rooms.

Far out at sea white and grey sails open to the wind were speeding homeward over the calm, silent, ominous water. Black spots—little motorboats—farther out, optimistically hoping for one last bite, slowly raised their lines and started toward shore.

At four-thirty the storm struck. Rain pelted down in torrents. It lashed the windowpanes. Water dripped through the roof. Rivulets coursed below doors and windows. The Station rocked, beds swayed, windows rattled, and puffs of smoke belched from the kitchen stove, doors banged and the wind whistled and shrieked round every corner. It was not yet nightfall but I had to light a lamp. With the darkness conquered, fear left me. Like the Rock of Gibraltar the building had stood the first impact. Safe inside, the ruthless blasts could not harm me.

All night the gale raged and the booming echoes of the waves thundering against the rocks filled the inky night. No boat could survive such a storm. Should a stray boat be caught at sea some children would be fatherless, some wife, a widow.

No one would venture outside because the force of the gale would carry him across the rocks into the sea. Annie would not return, I was sure, so at ten o'clock I dampened the fire, bolted the front door to prevent a flooded hall, and went upstairs to bed. Our kitchen door was always left unlocked so that urgent messengers could come in and shout to us from the foot of the stairs. But this night I thought I could sleep without a listening ear because no one would come. For half an hour I read *The Silk Stocking Murder*, then extinguished my coal oil lamp and dropped to sleep.

At midnight the sudden hush wakened me. A dead calm prevailed over land and sea. Another gale over, I thought, I wonder what damage awaits the morning? Then I went to sleep again.

At three o'clock a scuffling of wet boots against rocks again wakened me. I heard the back door open and a voice shouted upstairs, "Sister, Ise come for yous. A baby case." I breathed a prayer of thanksgiving that this baby had waited until the storm abated, and crawled from my warm bed into my oilskins, boots, and sou'wester. In the kitchen, Mr. Jones had lighted a lamp. As I went into my office he called to me, "Dress warm, Sister, outside, the sea shes wonderful." "Outside" meant deep water beyond Mutton Bay point. That point always spelled seasickness for me. I gulped, then left a hastily penned note propped against the kitchen lamp, telling Annie where she might locate me if I were needed.

In the shed, pools of water glistened in the moonlight. Outside, my boots squashed and oozed at every step, yet it was hard to realize that a terrific storm had recently swept through the village. Birds cheeped their morning welcome, gentle waves softly swished the shore. Although waning, the moon and stars lighted the sky. All nature was clothed in early morning freshness and beauty.

Coast fashion, Mr. Jones strode ahead of me carrying my kit. I swung my flashlight from side to side to prevent a misstep in treacherous cracks and on slippery rocks and tried hard to keep up with him. Daylight in August comes very early in Labrador; faint streaks of dawn were already creeping along the eastern horizon; everything was coming to life. It seemed a fitting time for a birth.

Wakened by Mr. Jones' motor coming into the harbor, fishermen knew someone was in trouble and their keen ears recognized the engine's individual notes. As we chugged past the homes, men came to the doors, stretched, gazed about, hitched up their trousers, and dragged on sweaters. Each one wondered what damage was just beyond his sight.

Dogs lazily stretched their paws, yawned, shook themselves, then slowly rose to their hind legs. With noses skyward, they saluted the dawn with their customary wolf-howl. Birds cheeped louder; gulls, balanced on one foot on the rocky cliffs, wakened, raised one wing, then the other, stretched their cramped legs, soared upward, and screamed a welcome to the morning.

When we reached the wharf Mr. Jones swung me lightly over the edge of the boat. Then, with one leap, he landed beside me. The motor sputtered, whirred, turned over, and we were away.

Curled up in the stern, I drank in the beauty as mauve-purple clouds faded to pinky-red, then burst into flaming orange as the sun crept up from the horizon.

It was quite evident that the storm had left a wake behind it. Before we reached that dreaded Red Bay point, the water became "loppy" and tossed our boat sideways, then pitched it forward as it lifted the bow out of the water. Green water sucked us down and then a great wave hurled us into the crest of the next one and we spanked down on the breakers. The thud shivered the boat from aft to stern. Finally a bigger wave picked us up and tossed our boat around the point into smooth water. The boat stood on end, heaved, pitched, and lurched. I clung to the edge, retching and vomiting. At that moment I was not blessing the nursing profession or newborn babies.

The thud of our boat as it bumped Mr. Manning's fishing stage put an end to my sufferings. Mr. Manning grabbed my kit. I tagged behind him over the rough, shaking board walk. When he reached the door of his home he plunked my bag down inside and exclaimed, "They'll show yous what yous wants," and disappeared.

Both expectant grandmothers left the young expectant mother upstairs and rushed down to welcome me. Apparently their hair had received a quick slick-up. As they came forward they drew on spotless aprons.

Young Mrs. Manning had no home of her own. According to custom, she had moved in with her husband's parents until such time, if ever, she and her husband could get a home of their own. If they did not succeed in this, when his parents passed away they would inherit the old home, feather beds, quilts, and all the household chattels.

One of those familiar drum-shaped, wood-eating kitchen stoves, with an oven front and wide ash pan, had been crammed with dry birchwood. Both sides were red-hot and emitted a terrific heat. On top, two teakettles hissed and steamed.

A wizened, weather-worn man, sitting with his chair tilted back, his feet on the ash pan, and a winter cap tightly pulled over his head, grunted a welcome. His heavy, home-knitted sweater was buttoned to his chin and his thick woollen trousers snuggled into huge gum rubbers. Probably between sixty and seventy, he looked as if he had weathered ninety years. A skunk-like aroma from his tobacco-stained wooden pipe saturated the air. Between puffs, he rolled his tongue around a wad of tobacco. To ease the situation, he leaned forward, squirted a string of brown juice into the ash pan, replaced his pipe, and picked up the tail of the last puff. (I have never been able to fathom how old-timers manage to smoke and chew at the same time.) Contented with the world, he kept muttering to himself, "A lot of foolishness. Too much fuss. All this commotion. What's a baby?"

A deep-throated growl from the dark depth near the window warned me to keep my distance. The quill hairs on the back of a wolflike bitch stood upright. Her drawn-back lips revealed sharp fangs, while her wrinkled upper lip indicated no quarter given. Three fuzzy-haired black balls with round, bulging tummies wiggled their stubby tails as they shoved and rooted for their breakfast. "Don't mind hern. Herns not vicious," exclaimed Mrs. Manning. "Give me your coat and mitts. Is'll be putting em by the stove to dry." I hoped they would not be put too close to the squirting stream of juice.

I started to sit on a chair at the other side of the kitchen to remove my rubber boots and put on my shoes, but halted in mid-air when Mrs. Tyler shouted, "Mind the baby!" It was dark, my glasses were frosted, and I had not noticed the floor. Beside the chair, his fat thumb in his tiny mouth, his head resting on a wadded-up black sweater, baby Tommy slept soundly. Beside him lay an empty liniment bottle with the top encased in a rubber nipple. Three flies perched on the tip of the nipple as they sucked at the last sticky drops.

The other corner of the room looked safe so I sat down on a homemade bench, but even here a heavy, pungent, greasy odor permeated my nostrils. My nose directed me to the wall where two big seals with smooth, sleek sides dripped blood and water. Their faces, like little old men, peered at me. The seals had commenced to run and the men had not had time to skin these. Left outside, they would freeze too solid to be skinned, so they had been brought, half-frozen, into the hot kitchen where they would be safe from the dogs until the men could work at them. The skins would be removed in this same corner and the meat cut up for home consumption. The entrails and blubber would be dragged across the floor, the blubber taken to the seal oil foundry, and the entrails ravenously devoured by the dogs.

Between the stove and the seals stood a large wooden barrel full of icy water. Above it, suspended from a nail in the wall, hung the family and company tin dipper. The barrel would stand there, open to dust, flies, and germs, from fall to spring. When the dipper scraped the bottom, more water would be carried from a pond on the rocks and dumped into it.

Memories of our spotlessly white, sterile caseroom and delivery room flitted through my mind. This would have to be my sterile water, dipped into the kettle, boiled on the stove, and carried upstairs. This barrel water and family wash basin, its greasy water-line marks washed off with the slop cloth and scalded, would be my sterile outfit. Later, by the hot kitchen oven, evading brown squirts, I would bathe the new arrival in the same washbasin. When finished, I would share a delicious, appetizing seal pie or stewed seal meat cut from those friendly seals in the corner.

I gave thanks for a strong stomach and good digestion.

Much more quickly than it takes to relate, I had unburdened myself of surplus clothing and donned my shoes and uniform. Mrs. Tyler had gone upstairs to her daughter so I picked up my kit and followed Mrs. Manning through the narrow, low door, up the steep, winding stairs, which ended in a small bedroom. Alice lay deep in a goose-feather tick on a low, double bed covered with two heavy, hand-pieced, homespun quilts. This chubby, freckled-faced, redhaired eighteen-year-old girl was little more than a child. Mrs. Tyler sat on the edge of the bed, holding her daughter's hand. A spasm of pain crossed Alice's face and her mother comfortingly and assuringly rubbed her back as she crooned, "Tis all right now. Sister's here. Yous'll be all right. Won't hern, Sister?"

"Sure," I replied, "everything is fine. It will not be long now." A pleased smile spread over Alice's face. I must not fail her.

One glance at Alice's face told me there was not much time to spare. I glanced about the bedroom. Two dust-laden, dog-eared hooked rugs were on the floor. The only stand or table was covered with a dusty scarf, and littered with a water jug, toilet articles, men's socks and ties, hairpins, and comb. If I disturbed anything there would be a cloud of dust and germs. I decided to contrive a makeshift chair-table for my sterile equipment.

Another spasm twisted Alice's face; she smiled wanly, then, exhausted, dropped back on the pillows. There was no time for further inspection. Both grandmothers dashed for the narrow stairs to get a washbasin and teakettle. Having seen the kettle boiling, I knew all germs were frizzled.

I placed the kettle on the floor by the chair, ready for instant use, sponged the basin with disinfectant and boiling water, flung the contents into the slop pail, filled the basin with sterile water, and set to work.

Between spasms, Alice told me that she had been on the hill picking bagh apples. The Labrador gale had hastened her home. Dead tired, she went to bed with her mother's superstitious notions ringing through her mind: "If yous gets frightened, lass, yous'll lose your baby." "Never run over rocks, it'll mark the baby." "Stooping and bending twists the unborn child." During the past months, she had listened to these frequent cautions but had disobeyed all three of them.

Very soon there was a nine-pound grandson for the two

grandmothers to exclaim over. Certain that there must be deformities, they minutely scanned the new arrival, but much to their surprise and I almost think, disappointment, their superstitions had failed them. After they had satisfactorily settled the ancestral resemblances, Mrs. Tyler brought Alice a mug of boiled black tea and a hunk of bread and lard. While she ate this we gathered around the kitchen table and enjoyed seal meat saturated in seal oil thickened with flour. Washed down with lye tea, the enzymes, juices, and blood-builders of this meal gave us all new energy.

Three hours later I left instructions with the relatives and set out for home. On his return, Mr. Manning would go out fishing, the new mother would rest a couple of days, then catch up with her neglected sewing and mending.

Coast women disregard nursing instructions about baby routine. The baby would nurse when he cried because, according to grandmothers, all crying babies are hungry, or why do they cry? At night, he would lie tucked between mother and father, cozy and warm, and all would sleep until the baby wakened unpleasantly damp and hungry. The mother would draw her baby to her and satisfy the hunger pains, then all would go back to sleep until morning.

In Labrador, babies mature extremely young. In a few weeks they are eating from a spoon. At eleven months one of my babies was walking over the rocks. The strongest carry on the race. Ample witness to this statement is given by the parish register of infant mortality and by dozens of tiny graves. After fifteen years' medical experience on the Coast, Dr. Grenfell is said to have stated that one in every three of the babies died before it reached the age of one year. Conditions have somewhat improved since then, but the infant mortality rate is still alarmingly high.

In many cases, the five to nine days' rest at childbirth is the only holiday girls and women have from an early age to death. Frequently women would tell me what they planned to do on their holiday in bed. Knitting, sewing, and reading material had been put away to be brought out the day after their babies came.

FAMILIARITY breeds contempt; practice develops confidence.

By September my shaky-kneed days were forgotten. During my first weeks in Mutton Bay sleep would not come as my mind mulled over such questions as: Would a doctor have done differently? Had I done everything possible for that human life? Now, deep sleep awaited me as soon as my head sank into my eiderdown pillow.

On September fifth, my subconscious mind suddenly told me that someone was hovering near me. Sleepily, I dragged my eyes open to confront an apparition. Annie was bending over me, enveloped in her oversized flannellette nightgown. Her corkscrew rag curlers stood upright as if with urgency. "Oh, Sister," she wailed. "The doctor's boat shes comin into the harbor. What'll Ise do? The fire bes not lighted. My curlers! Who'll go to the door?"

Before she finished her lamentations my feet struck the floor. "Hurry, we can be downstairs before they get here."

Never tell a Coast person to hurry unless you wish to invite disaster. Annie jumped back, tipped over and upset my water jug, and water coursed in all directions.

I grabbed my wrap-around uniform, twisted my hair into a sort of tidiness and buttoned my apron as I went downstairs. When the doctor opened the door I was there to greet him. With him was a stranger whom he introduced as the travelling dentist, Dr. Morris. No, they had not eaten breakfast. Would it be long? Fifteen minutes, at most.

We hurried to make coffee and toast for them, since the doctor was in great haste to be gone. As soon as breakfast was over, he left for his eastern trip and Dr. Morris, a thickset, chubby, muscular man, began to unpack his equipment.

I had thought my office crammed to capacity. Now with treasures from the fathomless depth of the dentist's bag, it overflowed. Plaster, impressions, spatula, mixing bowl, basin, rubber sheet, forceps, and novocain were everywhere. He held up a handful of forceps, uppers, lowers, molars, syringes, and sponges. In consternation he gazed at the bulky equipment bag at his feet and back to the overflowing tables, then he shoved his bag under the table with his foot, while with his empty hand he contrived a clear space on the table.

Annie brought a teakettle full of boiling water. The dentist turned to her. "Get a wide-topped spittoon. They spit wide." Not being a tobacco chewer, I had no spittoon, but after scratching her head for a moment, Annie disappeared and returned with a wide-mouthed, enamel slop pail. Soon I discovered that they spit high as well as wide. In front of the slop pail, Dr. Morris arranged a low-back chair, took out his syringe, and commenced to mix up some novocain. I had never worked with a travelling dentist and did not know what to expect. Suddenly, Dr. Morris turned and announced, "Ready." I went to the hall and shouted, "First!"

Dr. Morris stood waiting. Mr. Galliway, the first victim, six-feet tall, bony, and straight as a ramrod, stalked through the door, strode to the chair, hung his grey cap on the chair knob, and sat down. He curled his long legs around the chair legs, threw back his head and opened his mouth. I stood in front of him and looked into that awful, yawning cavity. Rows of blackened stumps with gaping, rotten holes in the center confronted me. I could think of nothing but fire-charred tree stumps with decayed cores.

They were terrible teeth—or rather, remnants of teeth—and the next fifteen minutes or so were dreadful for all three of us. I marvelled at the dentist's dexterity and strength but even more at the patient's endurance. After one brief interval when he got rid of the blood in his mouth he enquired calmly, "How many more, Doc?"

I thought he had reached the end of that remarkable endurance. Myself, I felt as if I could not stand another tussle followed by the sickening crunch of decayed bones.

"Four more."

"Go ahead, Doc."

When four more blackened hulls were safely out, Mr. Galliway cleansed his mouth, stood up, took his cap off the chair, and remarked, "Ise mustn't keep yous because there be lots waiting. How much?"

"Fifty cents," replied Dr. Morris.

Mr. Galliway dragged out a dogeared, homemade sealskin purse, tipped it upside down on the palm of his hand and out fell four pennies, two nickels, three dimes, two quarters and a handful of rank-smelling tobacco. Carefully, he sorted out the two quarters, wiped off the tobacco, handed them to the dentist, and muttered, "Much obliged." Relieved and satisfied, he walked out.

"Next," called the dentist. I stepped to the door and repeated, "Next." Annie, in the kitchen echoed, "Next." Before Mr. Galliway reached the outer door, the second victim was in the chair.

All day long, with half an hour off for lunch, we hauled out teeth. Men, women, and children who had suffered tooth troubles for months or years came from harbors round about. When darkness set in we kept on pulling by the light of a coal oil lamp. At last, all the patients had been taken care of. All except Donnie. Screaming at the top of his lungs, this four-year-old fisherman-in-the-making had been brought by his father. Mr. Benny and I managed to inveigle him into the chair but to keep him there until the dentist could remove the offending tooth was another task. When Dr. Morris reached for his forceps, Donnie streaked from our grasp like a greased pig and with a leap was out of the chair, through the door, and headed for home. Arrived there he crawled through a small hole in the foundation under the house beyond our reach, where he huddled until late that night when, tired and hungry, he crawled out. Early the next morning he darted back to his haven and stayed there until the "tooth man" left the harbor. At four Donnie already showed signs of the patience and endurance I had observed that day. Unfortunately it was misdirected, for it would be at least one year, possibly two, before a dentist again visited Mutton Bay.

Occasionally every Off-coaster succumbs to an overpowering longing for some trivial city luxury. After a fashion, I had managed a daily sponge bath, but one day an irresistible longing for a hot tub swept over me. I recalled how nightly, when I came off duty, I used to step into a steaming tub of water. Like Esau, perhaps I now would have sold my birthright for such a tub of soapy water.

In order to satisfy my craving, two boys agreed, for twenty-five cents each, to carry the water from our pond, a quarter of a mile away. With two small buckets each they trudged up the rocks. Annie hauled out our every-purpose copper wash boiler, which she placed on the kitchen stove over a roaring birch fire. I carried up the zink washtub and placed it on the hand-hooked rug in the center of my bedroom. I did not dare chance privacy in the kitchen, because at any moment a visitor or patient might pop in without knocking.

The boys returned with their pails of water, which teemed with what The Health Department terms "invisible algae," and other living things such as bacilli and bacteria. Hundreds of visible wigglers squirmed about, while on the surface leaves and stems chased each other inside their circular confines.

A bath was going to be more complex than I had anticipated.

Now I understood why Coast people did not bathe daily and why the doctor had warned me against giving male patients too many baths.

I made a wiggler-net of three thicknesses of gauze and stretched it across the wash boiler. Back and forth trudged the boys. When they emptied their last bucket I had a boiler full of water and a strainer full of wigglers. I had lived on the Coast long enough to know that nothing should be wasted, so with a sober face I asked Annie casually, "How do you cook wigglers?" "Oh, Sister," she exclaimed, "wes don't eat wigglers!"

A bucketful at a time, Annie and I carried the water upstairs. Never before had plain hot water held such an attraction. At the moment that luxurious hot tub was more tempting than a million dollars. Gingerly, I plunged in one foot, then the other, until feet and body were immersed; and although the twenty-four inch tub was far from comfortable, I was soon offering a thankful prayer just for hot water. After a soapy wash and a brisk rubdown I glowed with satisfaction.

When there was plenty of rainwater, without too many wigglers, worms, and leaves, a bath was one of the looked-forward-to summer luxuries. In winter, the water might congeal into ice during the bath.

Labrador clouds are apt either to withhold water altogether, or to send it forth in superabundance. A cloudburst followed by several days of downpour made miniature lakes about the Station and village. I squish-squashed from home to home. Everywhere old-timers greeted me with, "Ise never did sees nothing like this in all my days." Our attic was flooded and tubs were set out to catch the overflow in the hall; the shed was a swimming pool. Annie went about bemoaning this waste of water so I suggested that she put a sign outside the door: "Attic, private bath—a shilling; hall, semi-private bath—ha'penny; shed, no privacy—free." She threw up her hands. "But, yous wouldn't let no ones undress in our shed, would yous? Why, that would be wonderful scandalous!"

Annie's sense of humor was strictly limited. But her use of the word "wonderful" to describe my shocking suggestion was typical of Coast speech. A wonderful catch of fish might mean a very good or a very poor catch. Wonderful weather might mean bad weather or good weather. And a person might be said to be getting well, wonderfully well, or very sick, wonderfully sick.

For days the salt sea roared at our doors while men in rain-soaked slickers and sou'westers carried water from the hill. Finally the storm ceased during the night and at five o'clock the next morning an uncanny quiet wakened me. I raised the window blind and could see the tickle, with the water rippling in the breeze. Dew and hoarfrost sparkled on the rocks and grass. Above, the sliver of moon was fading, but Mercury still twinkled beneath it. Gradually the first rays of sun burst above the horizon. Relaxed in my feather bed, watching the dawning of another day, I felt it was grand to be alive.

The quiet hour for daydreaming suddenly ended with a soggy thud of wood bumping rubber, followed by dozens of wolflike howls echoing across the cove. At this time of the morning the arrival of a boatman meant trouble. I saw two men walking Stationward, but they did not have a patient or stretcher. Perhaps someone needed medicine, though this was not likely. One of the men knocked on the shed door. Annie stuck her head out the bedroom window and shouted, "Come in!" The rocking chair creaked and there was silence until Annie dressed and went down. Had it been a rush case they would have called upstairs to me. Perhaps this was an emergency without rush. Unless men came for a baby case or an extremely bad accident, it was customary to sit and visit a few moments with Annie. Then, the messenger would ask, "Sister in?" Always Annie asked, "Do yous want to see herns?" Always she knew they did, but she would ask this question a dozen times a day. Sometime in her lifetime they might say "No."

I slipped into the dining room and started to eat my breakfast when I heard Annie ask, "Do yous want hern?" A man's voice whispered, "Hern eating herns breakfast?" Annie replied, "Herns eating." "Let hern finish," he replied. Silence reigned while I finished and went to my office. Then Annie whispered, "Herns in there now." The chair creaked, rubber boot tops flapped, and heavy footsteps came slowly down the corridor. A young man whom I had never seen stepped into the office, sidled to a chair, sat down, and said, "Good morning, Sister. Nice morning."

He took off his cap, and shuffled his feet before stating, "Wes come for yous for Mrs. Casey."

He looked barely nineteen, shy, and reluctant to impart any information, and I knew it would take time to extract the facts in order to know what to take—medical, surgical, or maternity kit.

"Who is Mrs. Casey and from what harbor have you come?" I queried.

"Ise Jack Reddy and herns my neighbor. Theys no boat so Sam and me wes come to bring yous."

"What is her trouble?"

"Ise don't know, but herns is in bed suffering wonderfully."

"Has she pain in her side or her head?"

"Herns has pains all over hern's body, mostly hern's stomach, and hern's legs are swollen like stovepipes so hern can't walk."

Most Coast boys know life from conception, birth to death so I knew there would be little embarrassment if I asked a direct question.

"Is she going to have a baby?"

"Oh no, not for months, but herns that way, and something inside hern's stomach has gone wrong."

I knew what to take and that I must be prepared to be away hours or days.

By now the sun was high above the horizon and it was an ideal fall morning. A gentle breeze rippled the water but no life stirred in the village. This was unusual, because ordinarily at this hour fishing boats were going out or returning. The storm had changed all routine.

Wrapped in a rubber coat, curled up in the stern, daydreaming and speculating on the nature of this case, I watched the calm, transparent water skimming past. Prayer and faith are much greater fortifiers for an emergency than worry. Under the early sun, in the invigorating and nippy salt air, on the vast silent water, petitions for guidance and strength seemed natural.

Mrs. Casey certainly was in a bad way and something had to be done immediately. This time there were no friendly grandmothers, water barrel, or warm home. She was three months pregnant and had had complete retention for twenty-four hours. My only hope of giving temporary relief was to apply hot packs over her entire body.

She was lying on filthy quilts on a sagging board bunk in

a rickety two-room shack. The floor cracks were so wide I could see the damp mud below. Everything about the shack indicated a lazy husband. It was destitute even of the barest necessities. Several children crawled over the rough, cold floor. Mrs. Casey's husband was nowhere to be seen and apparently not interested in my diagnosis.

In the kitchen was a stove and a greasy, grey enamel family washbasin-cooking-tin. A few red embers sputtered in the stove. Outside, I found some green, wet tamarack which smouldered, then caught to a blaze. In the yard I dipped up a can of stagnant water. In order to bring the water to a boil, I took a newspaper from my bag and covered the washbasin.

Too sick to care what happened, the mother consented to treatment. At the bedside I wrung out most of the water from an old flannelette blanket. The water trickled through the floor while I quickly wrapped her in the steaming makeshift hotpack and encased her in heavy quilts. Almost immediately she felt relief, but all I could expect was temporary results.

After two hours' treatment it was apparent that she should be taken to the Station so I asked the eldest boy where I could find his father. He pointed his finger across the tickle and muttered, "Es probably over there pickled." The boatman had disappeared. I felt as stranded as Robinson Crusoe. Between the mainland and me, out on the high tide, our boat floated calmly indifferent to our need. Even if a kinoo had been available, the children were too small to send across.

I cupped my hands and shouted to a man on the other side of the tickle, "Are Mr. Casey and my boatman over there?" "Sure," he shouted back, "Ise'll send them over." An hour elapsed and no one showed up. I started to the shore, intending to give someone a piece of my mind, but I saw my boatman pushing off in a kinoo. When he reached land Mr. Casey, uncombed and unshaven, with a hangdog expression and shiftless eyes, grunted, "How do." Immediately I knew explanation to him would be useless. Raw truth might soak in so I said, "If you keep your wife here she will die. At the Station I will try to save her." Under his breath he cursed, then snarled, "Ise has no use for doctors or nurses. Neighbors said I neglected hern. That's why Ise sent for yous. No missus of mine shall be separated from her children. Hern stays and yous stays."

I had discovered that the only way to deal with such domineering hulks of humanity was to ignore them, so I turned to Jack Reddy and said, "You have heard my diagnosis. If Mrs. Casey dies here, I may have to charge her husband with manslaughter. I am ready to start home."

"All right, the tide is low," replied Jack.

I had banked on Mr. Casey yielding when he discovered himself cornered. He gave me a surly, menacing leer and threatened, "Yous can't leave her here to die."

We kept on toward the shore but when halfway there he came slouching up to us and muttered, "Take her along."

I went back, picked up the baby, then the older children, and held them up to kiss their mother good-bye, perhaps forever. She said she had a thirteen-year-old daughter somewhere in the village whom she had not seen for two days. Jack said he would send someone to locate her, and with the help of neighbors they would care for the children.

By now the tide was fifty feet from the shore so we wrapped Mrs. Casey in a quilt and her husband carried her out to the boat; Jack turned up his hip rubber cuffs, gathered me in his arms, waded out, and hoisted me after her.

On the way Mrs. Casey became deathly seasick. We cut the waves at that awful point and the stuffy cabin, gasoline odors, fish and human smells made the air thick and almost unbearable.

At the Station a comfortable, clean bed, a hot cup of tea, and sympathy took a weight from Mrs. Casey's mind. She needed immediate treatment but after what she had gone through it would be inhuman. Instead, a strong sedative gave her relief and she fell into a deep sleep from which she did not waken till midnight.

To give a hot pack in a hospital requires two or three nurses, rubber sheets, icecap, woollen blankets, and a tub of boiling water near the bedside. Two nurses wring the blankets and wrap them quickly around the patient while another keeps her finger on the patient's pulse and gives stimulating drinks. But here a zinc tub full of hot water was the only equipment. Mrs. Casey squatted in the tub, Indian fashion, while I gathered the quilts about her shoulders and held them over the edge of the tub so that her body would absorb all the steam. Soon, tiny globules of perspiration glistened on her forehead and trickles of salty poison ran down her face and neck. Her steaming moist body lost its parched appearance; our makeshift pack had not failed us.

For more than an hour I sat beside her and replenished the water, then we lifted her into bed and gave her an alcohol rub. The immediate danger was over. Her emaciated body relaxed and she slept for twelve hours. This was one of the many times I longed for a hospital, medical care, proper food, and sympathetic nurses. Two weeks later another emergency patient needed the bed, so much to my regret Mrs. Casey had to be sent back to her so-called home.

ONE day in October Uncle John came over with a suggestion, "Sister, Ise think yous would be wise to be cleaning your stovepipes and putting up all your winter stoves. It gets wonderful cold here in a hurry, sometimes overnight. Ise'll come over in the morning and help yous."

My training had not included the setting up of stoves but I presumed Sister Martin had done it and I could not mar the reputation of the Mutton Bay nurse.

The next morning, Uncle John, Annie, and I carried and rolled the heavy Quebec heater up the shed steps into the sitting room. With barked thumb, a skinned shin, and blood oozing from my knuckles, I finally saw the sitting room stove reposing in the right place.

"Yous just take the upper pipe and Ise'll take the lower kitchen ones and wes'll empty em," suggested Uncle John.

When we stepped outside, the wind swept through the open end of my pipe and covered me from head to foot with soot. Uncle John, with his customary chivalry, did not smile, but remarked sympathetically, "Plain to see yous never did carry a stovepipe." He laid his pipe on the ground and patiently gave me my first lesson in stovepipe carrying.

"Never think there is no wind. Always imagine the wind is blowing and carry the pipe sideways," he instructed. Many times since, that lesson has saved me a sooty face.

The steamer whistle blew. "Herns in," exclaimed Uncle John. "Ise has to go." He dropped the pipes on the living room floor and disappeared through the doorway. Rather than walk around and over those pipes for several days, Annie and I decided we would make an attempt to put them up.

I slipped on a disreputable dress and a pair of huge pigskin gloves and climbed up on the mantel shelf. With one foot on the shelf and the other on the back of a chair, I reached for the pipes. Annie stood below and steadied the chair and me. As we raised the last length the ceiling wire gave way and four lengths of pipe clattered to the floor spraying soot in all directions. Footsteps sounded on the gravel walk outside the window. Annie shouted, "The clergyman be coming with two strangers!"

I had spent weeks drilling Annie into ways of tidiness. With her inborn hospitality and my training in her mind, she took her hand off my chair and grabbed the broom. I was left in the air, with my legs two feet apart, balancing between the chair and mantel shelf—not a very dignified position from which to welcome strangers. The vibration of the bang of the door jarred the pipe from my hand and upset my equilibrium. I plunged headlong to the floor just as the strangers entered the room. The new clergyman's sense of humor saved the day and introductions were made amid much laughter. Mr. Cragg introduced himself as Mr. Moak's successor—he was to make Mutton Bay his headquarters for some time—and the student priest with him as Mr. LeMont, who would spend the winter farther west. The other stranger, Miss Daniels, was a volunteer worker, a young university student direct from a large American city. She had come to live with me for the winter and do community work.

Annie and I put away the pipes until a more convenient time while Miss Daniels was initiated into life at Mutton Bay. Saturday morning Mr. Cragg persuaded her to play the organ for the Sunday service.

"I tried the organ last night," Miss Daniels said on the way to church Sunday morning. "I am not certain whether I can make my feet and hands work at the same time. Already my knees are knocking together."

But she entered the schoolhouse-church bravely enough and took her place on the wobbly organ stool.

At first, in spite of one squeaky key and a pedal that required lubricant, all went well. Then, in the middle of the first verse, one key stuck. Miss Daniels gave it a jab and out it came but continued to emit a whistling, squealing noise. As is the custom, she paused, then gave the starting note. Everybody rose but no one joined Miss Daniels. Expecting every moment that the congregation would join her solo, she played the first verse through again. Encouraged at having mastered the organ, she tackled the second verse boldly and confidently, certain that now they would join her. Although the organ behaved like a queen, the congregation remained dumb.

As she played the last line of the second verse, Mrs. Leeds, a forthright little woman, went up to her and whispered loudly, "Wes don't knows that tune. If yous'll play this one and start over again wes'll sing with you."

Thankful to know the reason for the holdup, Miss Daniels changed the tune and every voice joined her until the rafters rang with joyful hallelujahs. Faster and harder worked Miss Daniels' feet. Louder squealed the stuck key. Higher rose the voices, some, like mine, out of tune, some ahead or behind the music. But I am certain the good Lord makes allowances for off-note singers. Happy and satisfied we went home to enjoy our dinner.

On Monday morning we still had to confront those awful pipes. Determined not to climb over them any longer, I went for Uncle John. He came at once but those cantankerous pipes seemed to be possessed with the devil. Once more, soot was tracked from the woodshed, through the kitchen, to the living room, and smoke belched from the double pipe connection. Uncle John chuckled, "There be nothing to putting up pipes . . . Yous climb up on the table and balance on the back of this chair and steady them. Ise'll do all the work."

Perched on the chair back, with smudges on my face and uniform, I did not hear the steamer enter the harbor on her homeward trip. The first intimation we had that the *North Shore* was in harbor was the sight of two strangers standing in the open door watching us.

This time I climbed down without mishap and met Dr. More and Miss Cress from Battle Harbour Hospital. They had been working in the Grenfell Mission Hospital there and were returning to their homes for the winter. This was the last steamer to connect with the northern harbor winter boat.

For several months they had lived on scant rations so I told them to crawl into our little cellar and choose what appealed to their tastes. In a few moments they came up with a pound tin of lobster. As they were swallowing the last mouthful, the steamer's whistle sounded across the water!

"Why! The steamer was to be in harbor for an hour or two unloading freight!" Miss Cress exclaimed in dismay. "We *must* catch it."

We fairly flew from the Station to the nearest fishing stage. There was no boat available to take us out to the steamer! Frantically we rushed from rock to rock, shouting and waving our arms, but could not attract anyone's attention. The second whistle blew, a signal to draw up the ladder and anchors. All passengers were supposed to be on board and all visitors off the vessel!

But Captain Legault spied us just in time. Proceedings were halted until Uncle John found and launched a small boat containing two grateful passengers.

A farewell wave and they were away. I went back to the Station, vowing that never again would I tackle stovepipes without first putting up a Scarlet Fever sign far enough from the Station so that we might see visitors before they saw us.

October slipped away as if on wings. Helping to bring new babies into the world and attending to a number of dysentery cases were added to the constant nursing in homes and at the Station.

On October twentieth, two boys strolled into the Station. They visited with Annie for half an hour then she came in to me and, in an excited voice, announced, "Theyse wants yous."

What for? I wondered. Just then I was not in a mood to yank another tooth, "born" a baby, or do a dressing.

Tommy clumped into the office, nodded his head, and greeted me with, "Yous all are invited to Ester's wedding tomorrow," then walked out before I had time to ask any questions. I now knew why Annie has been so excited.

"Us'll go, won't us?" Annie asked eagerly.

"Who is Ester? Where does she live? What does a wedding involve?" I questioned cautiously. Annie told me that each person invited took a cake or pie, a present, and herself to the wedding supper and dance that lasted the night through.

"Why didn't we receive our invitation sooner?" I asked.

In the course of the morning Annie satisfied my curiosity on this and many other points in connection with weddings on this isolated coast.

A bride must have suitable clothes. These usually have to be ordered from Toronto, Quebec, or Montreal weeks or months previous to a wedding. Should the clothes arrive too large or too small someone may be found who can make the necessary alterations. If not, the clothes have to be returned and another few weeks elapse before there can be a wedding. When the clothes are ready, a time is set that will not conflict with the run of the fish. It is extremely important that all nets and traps have attention at specified times. What good would a husband be to a bride if he could not feed her during the winter? Food for the wedding is another important item. This is a day for relatives and friends from all the near harbors to feast, visit, and dance.

When the bride has consented, when she has her clothes, when there is food, when it is not rush fishing, and when the day has been set, the clergyman is notified. He announces the banns at three services. As the eventful day draws near the relatives and friends of the bride go to her home and start cooking. After the banns have been published, should the clergyman arrive in the harbor before the expected date, a relative puts off in a boat to seek the groom-to-be. If he is ready and if he can spare time to get married, the wedding will take place immediately. If not, several weeks or months may elapse before the clergyman again visits the harbor.

Wedding invitations are issued by young men and boys called "bride's boys" who go from harbor to harbor, inviting the people as these boys had invited us today. At the time of a wedding, animosities are usually forgotten for the day. But sometimes it is decided that someone will not be invited. If so, when the boys approach a group of people and notice that person in the group they will say to each in turn, "Yous are invited to Mary's wedding," ignoring the one not to be invited. He will know the reason why he is omitted.

It was to a hastened wedding we had been invited on the morrow. The steamer had brought food and it would not keep. It also brought wedding clothes which fitted the bride and she was anxious to wear them. The banns had been published, but the clergyman had not been expected until next month. Now word had just been received that he would be in the village the next day and this might be his last trip for several weeks. The fishing season was over and it might be dirty weather very soon so the wedding was to be held the next afternoon.

Excitement prevailed throughout the village as dresses were pressed, bride's boys sent out with invitations, food cooked, and houses scrubbed, because visitors would be coming to nearly every home.

There was excitement at the Station too as we baked pies, pressed clothes, and prepared to remain away all night. Miss Daniels was thrilled at the thought of a new and unique experience. Annie was in a whirl because it meant being with her people and having the time of her life. I had already been up two whole nights that week with a baby case, so I was much less enthusiastic at the thought of sitting long hours in a crowded room permeated with the mingled odors of humans, dogs, sealskin boots, and food.

Annie's two-day work schedule was finished in half the time she usually took. By noon the next day, we all had suitable clothes to wear. When ten of us crowded into a small motorboat and left the harbor, I noticed that I was the only one with an overnight bag. I had put in my pyjamas, comb, and toothbrush, for, if opportunity arose, I intended to get a few winks of sleep. If there was sufficient privacy, I also intended to take off some outer woollens. The rest were prepared to dance the night through.

It was a beautiful day. The water was green, cold, and rough, but excitement prevented seasickness. We arrived at Ha-Ha Bay at two o'clock in the afternoon, one hour before the wedding.

The weather-beaten wooden school-church was on the bank of the tickle, half a mile from the bride's home. Ester, the bride, looking quite lovely, stepped out of her home with her white tulle wedding veil flowing far below her waist. A silver heirloom brooch held in place the orange blossoms which encircled her brow. As she left the house her cousin rang the church bell, and its voice echoed across the water. Leaning on her brother's arm (her father was not living) the bride sedately walked down the gravel path to the beaten single-file trail which wound in and out among the stunted spruce trees. Her brother, Mack, stepped ahead and tested the muddy spots. Close behind him, in her white shoes, Ester delicately picked her way and, like a long camel-train on a desert pilgrimage, we all followed. The furze caught Ester's flimsy veil on its sharp points; each time her other brother, behind her, patiently untangled it and the procession proceeded. Just before we reached the church, we had to cross fifty feet of water and stones. At high tide the salt water washed over this point. The wedding had been planned so that we could cross at low tide. When we came to this spot Mack stepped back, stooped, carefully gathered up Ester's flowing drapery and lifted her into his arms. High above the mud he jumped from rock to rock. When they came to a grassy plot near the church, he stood her on her feet and she climbed the steep bank.

All along the trail, as close as possible to her ears, men and boys had been shooting off their powder-loaded guns. A wedding, like a funeral, is an occasion in which young and old participate. School had been dismissed in order that the children might enjoy the event and so that the schoolhouse could be used as a church.

One by one we entered the church and then stood, wedged in like sardines; the men took off their caps and leaned their guns against the outside church wall. Since there was no altar, a Bible stand made from square upright posts stood near the tiny organ near the front of the church. Behind this the clergyman, Mr. Cragg, took his place as the groom marched up, turned, and stood with his back to us. On Mack's arm, to the strains of wedding music, Ester walked up the aisle, the two bridesmaids and the best men following. Then Mack stepped back and Tom, the groom, took his place beside Ester.

As Mr. Cragg read the service a hungry, wayward bee sought shelter in the warm church. Apparently it had forgotten that summer was gone, for when it saw the artificial blossoms it buzzed about Ester's head. Every eye focused on that bee. I began to wonder if Ester would scream, giggle, or faint. She did not blink an eye. Throughout the long service it buzzed until Tom reached for the ring to place on Ester's finger. This upset the bee. It lighted on Tom's ear and dug its stinger deep into his ear lobe. Tom, forgetting everything but the fiery dart, dropped the ring and threw up his hand to swat the bee. Away rolled the ring under Mr. Cragg's long black skirts. Boys tittered, girls giggled, and the atmosphere was charged with suppressed merriment. In a frantic effort to regain the ring, Mr. Cragg and Tom ducked at the same instant and their heads came together with a thud. The suppressed mirth overflowed. Mr. Cragg, the ring in his hand, straightened himself. He gave one stern glance at the congregation and a subdued hush fell as Tom took the ring and the service continued.

When the nuptial knot was satisfactorily tied, Mr. Cragg and the newlyweds signed the register. This gave the young men a chance to sidle through the crowd and pick up their guns. Ester left the church with the boom of gunpowder explosions tinging in her ears. The boys ran in front of her and kept firing whenever they could get close to her. Off and on until midnight an occasional bang was heard, interspersed with the ringing of the church bell.

Back at Ester's home we found long tables, laden with food, extending the length of two rooms. The bridal attendants stood waiting to serve the crowd. We sat on hard, homemade benches two or three deep along the walls of the kitchen and hall. Children and dogs squirmed about our feet, but the servers, holding steaming plates and carrying jugs of hot tea above our heads, managed to edge through the mob without mishap.

When the food was on the table the hostess called out the names of those who were to be honored at the first table.

"Mr. and Mrs. Mosley come and eat."

"Mary Ann come and eat."

She called until all the chairs were filled. When everyone at the table was satisfied that his stomach would not hold another crumb, he pushed back his chair and went to the bench. The dishes were whisked away, washed, put back, and the hostess continued calling names until all were served.

When the last person left the table there was a large quantity of food left. Between dances, as they felt the need, couples strolled over to the kitchen and had another snack.

Ester's home was so small a relative had offered his home for the dancing. The crowd pushed their way outside and we could hear the rhythmic music of a violin and an accordion; as we entered we could hear the fiddlers keeping time with their feet while one man mounted the table and shouted:

"All promenade."

"All change."

"Birdie swing in and hawk swing out."

"Balance all."

Early in the evening Mrs. Roberts, a woman whom I had previously treated, whispered, "Ise going home early. If yous wish to goes with me no one will be offended. They'se knows yous has to work tomorrow." I appreciated her thoughtfulness but wondered what she would consider early.

When two o'clock came I was ready to drop on my feet and would willingly have crawled into any corner to catch fifty winks. Mrs. Roberts' "early" was late for me.

At three o'clock Mrs. Roberts whispered, "Ise going now." I followed her over the rough frozen ground and rocks to her home. Half asleep, I hauled off two sweaters and my skirt then pulled on my pyjamas over my woollens. With heavy quilts tucked about my neck, snuggled into a goose-feather bed, I forgot the world.

It seemed only a moment later that I felt someone tugging at my bedclothes. As I tried to rouse myself I could not recall where I was or what was wanted of me. Then I heard Mrs. Roberts saying, "Its jest me. Mr. Morton is here and he wants yous. The excitement has started his wife. Herns time has come and hern wants yous to come at once."

The weather had turned much colder. My teeth chattered and I shivered as I went out into the frosty night. Like great spiders, Mr. Morton's long legs flicked back and forth in front of his lantern. Once, when I lagged behind, he saw me struggling to keep up, came back, took my arm, swung his lantern behind him, and apologized for hurrying. "But," he said, "herns alone with Aunt Mary and Ise wants to get to hern." So did I but without a broken leg or neck.

Fortunately Mrs. Morton was young and had spent the early

part of the evening at the wedding, then walked home over the rough rocks. Soon another fisherman's daughter blessed the home. Both were fine, and the mother, baby, and family were going to bed to get some much-needed sleep. It was five o'clock when I went back to Mrs. Roberts' and tumbled into bed again.

At seven, Mrs. Roberts shouted through the door, "The boatman is here. John hes wants to be off right away because there be a heavy, wicked sea making outside, and it be getting wonderfully rough. Ise wants hes would wait until yous has a bite to eat but hes willn't." Cold, hungry, tired, and sleepy, once more I crawled out.

Fourteen weary men, women, and children huddled into our small motorboat. Soon it became apparent that John had made a wise decision. No boat would travel tomorrow or the next day.

Two miles out our boat headed straight into the teeth of a monstrous wave. The boat mounted high on the swell as green water rushed under and a beastly white-capped wave split over the stern. Icy salt water cascaded above us and drenched everything and everybody. Women screamed, "Us'll all be drowned! Plez! Plez! John, turn back!"

Mrs. Lyons dropped to her knees and started counting her rosary. Mrs. Mace begged John to go on because her husband was alone with her young baby. John knew if he turned back he would have to leave his boat in that harbor all winter. Also we would have to hike six miles over an almost impassable unbroken trail of rocks and portages. But to go on might mean death to all. The boat righted itself and, with a loud spank, struck the next wave. We rode the crest of a wild breaker and John calmly stated, "Wes'll go ahead." Each mile seemed longer and rougher than the preceding one.

Never before had Mutton Bay looked so comfortable, friendly, and welcoming. We had taken four hours to make six miles. It was eleven o'clock when Annie and I stepped out of our soaked clothes and dropped them on the kitchen floor.

No more Coast weddings that involved a night's stay for me!

THE last steamer of the fall brought our winter supplies. These were all we'd have until next June or July, when the ice and sea were sufficiently open for the steamer to enter the harbor again. It was absolutely necessary to check each precious piece of freight on the manifest as it was brought from the hold. Muffled in dickie and sealskin boots from scalp to toe, chilled to the marrow, I stood on the windswept *North Shore's* deck. At intervals we managed to step inside and warm our limbs until someone stuck his head through the door and shouted, "Your freight bes next, the purser wants that yous be ready to check." At five o'clock the last piece had been struck off the list. Uncle John informed me that he had stowed all our freight, as fast as it was unloaded, in his kitchen, away from dogs and frost. "Wes can't land freight at the Station until high tide at midnight," he said.

Stiff and cold, I swung down the rope ladder and jumped into Uncle John's boat. The captain shouted, "Raise anchor. All hands forward." A sailor hauled up the rope ladder, the engine started, and sailors hauled the anchor rope and wound it around the great iron posts on the deck. Uncle John shoved his boat away from the wash of the propeller and the *North Shore* swung westward while the crew shouted, "Have a good winter! See you next spring!"

And we replied, "Merry Christmas—to everyone!"

On the way home I made up my mind to have fifty winks of sleep before midnight. The cold air had made me very drowsy. More asleep than awake, I did dressings for patients who had waited two hours for my return, ate a hot supper, and crawled to bed. At eleven-thirty, Annie shouted, "There be the putt of Uncle John's motor!" Out in the darkness we caught sight of the flickering light of his lantern swinging in the stern. By now the wind had teeth. Two boatloads of freight drew into the wharf and anchored at our rocks. These rocks were slippery, steep, and treacherous, so I got out extra lights to take to the men. A drizzling, sleety rain greeted me when I opened the shed door. Uncle John fastened our lantern to a high post which lighted up the rocks between the boat and the Station, then he stretched a plank from the boats to the rocks. Knee deep in the chilling, briny water, regardless of cold and fatigue, with sleety rain slowing progress, the men went back and forth carrying loads of freight up to our kitchen. Under their heavy loads it was impossible for them to see all the trip holes in the rocks so I walked ahead flashing light in front of them.

The only means of summer transportation over land is a homemade carrier which consists of two poles with slats across them. If the load is extremely heavy it takes one man at each end of both of the poles; if lighter, only two men are needed. Patients, seals, coal, and all types of freight have to be carried this way.

By three o'clock in the morning the kitchen resembled a junk shop. When the men had finished their mugs of hot coffee and thick hunks of bread it was four o'clock. We went to bed until eight, then we started to pack away our year's supply of precious food. Fresh eggs would not be strictly fresh, and butter might be slightly off-flavor, but eggs are eggs although overripe, and butter is butter no matter how strong it smells or tastes. We felt rich, almost luxurious, as we contemplated our full cupboards.

The disappearance of the last steamer around the point was a signal for all routine to change. Sometime during the night summer melted into oblivion and winter took its place. By noon winter supplies were being moved into the homes where they would be safe from hungry dogs and destroying frost. For weeks nets and traps had been drying on the rocks; now they were carried inside ready to be repaired during some winter blizzard. Potatoes, meat, lard, oatmeal, flour, and vegetables in huge quantities were put into a primitive cellar, a hole under the kitchen floor.

As the weather grew colder, last minute boatloads of wood were thrown up on the rocks to be moved later by dog-team over the rocks to the homes. Sealskin boots replaced rubber ones, summer clothing was packed away, and heavy woollen socks, waterproof dickies and mittens appeared.

Almost every home has an outside summer kitchen in which the people live during the summer. Now, cookstoves, tables, chairs, dishes, and cupboards were moved into the winter kitchen. This inner room is the fisherman's sanctuary and living quarters until spring. Wood, komatics, dog harness, frozen seals, water buckets, and slop pails stay with the dog food in the summer kitchen.

Just as man's routine changed so did the harbor: barren black rocks and cold, green, lacy white-capped water disappeared, for during the next afternoon goose-feather snow fell steadily. By night the hillside was a world of sparkling, fleecy, white beauty. The water was a pudding mess of "slob"—ice and snow mixed and similar to unformed ice in an ice-cream freezer. Later this changed to a glare sheet of solid ice and, still later, to a soft, white-padded carpet. Winter in deadly earnest would soon be upon us.

All large boats require from ten to fifteen men to haul them from the water, over sand and rocks, far enough from the shore to prevent a tidal wave or huge, floating ice cakes destroying them. Boys scurried through the village hunting for men to "gang up" to haul boats to safety. And in less than a week summer was forgotten as the winter routine of dog-teams and komatics was established.

During the last part of November the thermometer dropped lower and the wind bit keenly as our building creaked and groaned with frost. This was my first experience with coal. Annie informed me that Sister always filled the Quebec heater with coal and closed off the dampers before going to bed. "Ise always finds red embers each morning," she declared. I must live up to Sister's reputation. At ten o'clock, before going upstairs, I dumped on a hod and a half of hard coal, shut the dampers tightly, and went upstairs confident that everything was all right and we would get up in a warm house in the morning. Half an hour after I went to bed a terrific explosion rent the air. For a moment I was too petrified to move or think. Then I remembered the Quebec heater. I lit a lamp and hurried downstairs. A blast of coal gas nearly blinded and choked me when I opened the living room door. The explosion had raised the top of the heater, released the gas, and then the top had settled back into place.

Annie, eyes bulging, and corkscrew rag curlers sticking out like porcupine quills, stumbled down the stairs in her nightgown. Horrified, she threw up her hands. "Oh, Sister, 'tis wonderful that wes be alive! Yous should have let off the gas before closing it up."

November and early December are "standstill" months. While harbor ice is catchin' (forming), it is impossible to move from harbor to harbor. Sickness in other harbors has to wait for safe ice and dog travel. Few babies are born during this period. Mothers know that no nurse can get to them and they will have to depend on their husbands or some woman in the village. If anything goes wrong probably both lives will be lost.

During standstill months the Station nurse is able to sandwich in community and social work, home-nursing classes, welfare visits, to teach pre- and post-natal mothers, conduct clubs, help with Red Cross work and oversee nursing.

Miss Daniels and I set to work to prepare our winter schedule. When a clergyman was in the village we attended Sunday services, but when no clergyman was available we planned to carry on with the Sunday school class.

There was no official barber in Mutton Bay, so we set aside Monday afternoon for haircutting. As an outlet for shut-in mothers and to help provide the Red Cross with articles, that evening we planned to have an undenominational Red Cross meeting in some home or the Station.

Miss Daniels, an excellent musician, decided to give several children music lessons at the Station on Tuesday afternoons. While this awful drumming on the organ (a new child each hour) was going on I could seek refuge in home-nursing visits.

There was a crying need for a Grenfell community club and hall so we set aside Wednesday evening to raise money for this purpose. Married and single, young and old, women could sew and knit for a sale. Miss Daniels was not a knitter or sewer but she was a remarkably good reader. Each week she would read a few chapters from an interesting book. She discovered if she closed at an exciting moment and said, "To be continued next week," many would return to hear the rest of the story. Some of the women could not read or write, and those who could had no time for reading. After the children were in bed, dozens of socks, mitts, and a pile of clothes waited to be darned and patched.

Thursday was our afternoon and evening off duty except for our own meals, stoking the fire, dishwashing, and answering the door.

On Friday afternoon the Junior Red Cross, consisting of children from four to fifteen years old, came to the Station and

I enjoyed teaching them to sew, knit, or make scrap books. We served cocoa and sandwiches and I had practically to push them out the door before darkness set in. After I had shooed them out, my head rang with, "Plez Sister, Mark took my thread;" "Plez, Ise can't make the knot go through;" "Plez, John wipes his pasty finger on me;" "Plez, Ise dropped a stitch," and always, "Plez show us the pictures you made."

The children were fascinated by my camera and swarmed about me when they saw me using it, pushing each other as they whispered shyly, "Ise first. Take me." Some of them had never seen a camera before and all were interested in how their pictures could get into the little black box. Long before the developed snapshots were ready the children would rap on the door, and when Annie answered the door the query was always the same, "Is my picture out of the black box yet?"

On Saturday morning every good housewife is supposed to clean her home. We must follow traditional routine. As a matter of fact I soon discovered that by Saturday the Station needed to be scrubbed from top to bottom, and supervising the cleaning was a full-time job. On Saturday night came the week-end luxury—a bath! Saturday evening, physically cleansed, spiritually refreshed, relaxed, and preparing a Sunday school lesson in front of a roaring fireplace, the difficulties and hard work of the week were forgotten.

A horse may balk, a car may stall, a bronco buck, but you can never foretell what a dog-team will do.

Smothering snow fell all night the thirtieth of November, so early the next morning men started to get their dog-teams in trim for winter work. Five to ten dogs are harnessed fanwise (wild goose V-shape). The best dog is called the leader dog and it is hitched to a sealskin trace thirty to fifty feet long in front of the komatic, a wooden sled made with two runners having steel shoes, with slats across the top on which a sitting-box is securely roped. This trace has a loop on the end which is slipped over a pivot rope attached between the two runners of the komatic. The leader dog forms the point of the V. The next-best two dogs, a few feet behind, are hitched to shorter traces one on each side. By twos, each pair widen the diameter of the V, until the last pair are a few feet ahead of the front runner points. Each dog wears a sealskin harness with the traces attached to it.

When the dogs are harnessed the driver collects all the loops and slips them over the pivot rope, which is securely fastened to the runners. Then the dogs are ready for action. In an emergency a quick pull of the looped rope instantly frees all the dogs' traces. The last pair, the poorest and laziest dogs, have to keep ahead of the sharp runners or get run over.

Although years have passed, my first komatic ride remains vivid in my mind. Miss Daniels and I stood on the Station steps and watched the men battling with the dogs. Puppies were being hitched for the first time. Young and old dogs were being taught to take their places in front of the komatics. Men were scraping rusty steel shoes with pieces of stone.

We had never seen a dog-team in action so, eager and fascinated, we watched the struggle of the squirming, yapping, seething mass of dogs, traces, and drivers. Suddenly, from the rocks above, eight dogs streaked in sight trailing a komatic and driver behind them. They scraped over the bare rocks, struck a snowbank, and whirled around the corner of the Station. Their driver, Tom, shouted, "If yous wants a ride jump on." Without stopping to think, we jumped on. The dogs whizzed around the corner of the Station and headed up the rocks. Miss Daniels desperately clutched my waist while I clung to the driver and the komatic.

We grated over mossy, frozen ground, sank deep into soft snowbanks, dipped into hollows between rocks, then skidded over icy spots as the dogs raced along. At the brink of a steep cliff we balanced high above our water pond. Without hesitating, the dogs catapulted down the steep bank and shot out onto the partially formed ice. Before we could think or act we were thrown from the komatic and stood waist deep in icy slob water. As I sank, I wondered how deep the pond would be and if there would be another layer of ice underneath to hold us. Also, who would notify my relatives? There *was* another layer and it held. The dogs wheeled and dashed back up the bank, where they stood waiting for us. We waded to the shore, jumped onto the komatic, grabbed the ropes, and raced back down the hills to the Station.

The next day, Mrs. Manning told me it was the first time Tom's puppies had been in harness. "Hes did not expect yous to accept," she said, "hes shouted as a dare." That ride gave us great prestige and was well worth the ducking.

Day by day the weather got colder and we added more blankets to our beds, another layer of newspapers beneath our mattresses, and pulled on an extra sweater when we went outside.

A Coast winter's morning always presented a challenge. At six o'clock, from under a mountain of blankets, encased in woollens, turtlelike I would stick out my head, give my nose a tweak to make certain it was not frozen, then draw back into my shell to recover from the shock. In a few moments I would gingerly stick out one bedsocked foot, then another, shiver, then finally emerge completely. Now the real ordeal commenced as I side-stepped a snowdrift to close the ventilator, if it were open, then leaped back to the icy linoleum. Quite frequently I did not open the ventilator because tiny mounds of snow sifted under and over the sills bringing plenty of fresh air with them.

Two feet from my bed a stovepipe came up from the office coal fire. Before retiring I placed my water jug, tooth paste, and wash cloth beside the pipe. Many times the water and paste were frozen solid. One morning Miss Daniels called me in to see her hand lotion. The cork, like a wee stovepipe hat, sat half an inch above the bottle on a streak of frozen lotion.

At four o'clock one morning my foot struck something wet and cold. On investigating I discovered that my hot-water bottle had leaked and my blanket was crisp with frost. In training we were never warned not to freeze patients with hot-water bottles!

Just before Christmas an emergency call came from a village six miles away. "The dogs had her down," was the message. That would probably mean that a child had fallen among the dogs and may have suffered twenty or thirty bites. I left by dog-team as quickly as possible.

My guess proved to be right and I spent several hours treating the wounds and calming the frightened little girl. I left directions and dressings with the mother and at two o'clock in the afternoon we set out for home. At three o'clock a Labrador gale showed in the offing. Far out at sea we could see black clouds rolling in, gathering force as they approached. The wind swept past us at forty miles an hour. Tom mushed, first with one foot then the other, in an attempt to urge the dogs to greater speed. He ran beside them shaking his snake whip and shouting,

"Eddy-up, eddy-up." I had to turn around and ride backwards so that the cutting wind could vent its force against my back. At five o'clock wet blinding snow filled the air and clung thickly to our hoods and dickies.

Suddenly on the brink of an open glade our dogs halted. Tom, with a quick jerk, unhitched the traces. With a leap, the dogs were over the glade onto floating ice. When they were safe on the other side they stopped, sank to their haunches, lapped snow, and rolled over in the drifts. Tom snatched up the pivot rope and shouted, "Hang on. Don't move. For the love of life, don't lose hold of the komatic." With a sickening shudder I realized why he had shouted, "Stick to the komatic." One second in the rushing water below us and I would have been sucked under the ice. Before I had time to think he jerked the nose of the komatic and it dropped with me on it onto the opposite floating ice.

Tom rehitched the dogs and urged them on faster. The gale was rapidly approaching when we came to a narrow dog trail, rounded in the center and sloping to icy sides. For three hundred feet the trail ran along within one foot of open, roaring rapids. As if by instinct, the dogs entered this trail, slowed down and cautiously felt their way. They seemed to know that one misstep would mean instant death. As they clawed their way along, a front paw would skid from the rounded center and dangle over the rushing water. With a scramble, the dog would frantically claw himself back onto the path, only to find his hind paw over the treacherous edge. One by one, the dogs reached the safe trail again and without stopping they looked back, as if to say, "We did it!" Then they strained their shoulders into their harnesses, lowered their heads into the oncoming storm, and raced on.

Coast dogs are a mixture of savagery and love. Given a chance they might devour a person in a few moments, yet the same dogs will undergo hardships and suffering, extreme cold and hunger, in an attempt to take one to safety.

Just as we reached the Station, the gale struck like the roar from a dozen cannons. The building shook, windows rattled furiously, and snow drifted into the kitchen. For a while it seemed as though the rafters would not hold against the fury of the storm. It was a wicked, wild night. Any babies ready to come into the world or any split heads would have to wait until morning.

Christmas in Labrador is the one festivity of the year. The days before the annual concert and Christmas Day so much time is spent in preparation—curling hair, pressing dresses, and cooking—that no one has time to think of aches and pains. This leaves the nurse free for a much-needed breathing spell.

We spent the day before Christmas decorating the schoolhouse. By night we had the platform erected for the amateur actors. As soon as supper was over, about five o'clock, young and old made for the schoolhouse. By seven o'clock it was packed to the doors. Parents with one or two children on their knees sat on the hard benches.

When everything was ready the schoolteacher announced, "Will yous all keep as quiet as possible so wes can hear. Wes will now begin."

Two boys tugged on the cord, the brown gingham curtain flew back, and the concert started. Amid peals of laughter and hand clapping, amateurs entertained a thrilled audience with recitations, dialogues, plays, and songs for two hours. The actors and actresses got as much pleasure out of their own acting as did their audience; when the audience laughed, they stopped acting and joined them; when the laughter subsided they continued where they had left off.

At nine o'clock we stood up and stretched our aching legs and in many different keys sang the national anthem. As the music died away the air was electric with expectancy. Children under five clambered over their parents and watched eagerly for the door to open. Those over five, sophisticated but excited, whispered to the tiny tots, "Ise hear hes. Santa's coming."

Suddenly nothing could hold the youngsters as they leaped up on the benches and shouted, " 'T is Santa." Dogs barked, bells jingled, and sealskin boots scuffed the boards. Then puffing and blowing his fingers, shaking off the snow, Santa stepped through the door. He nodded his head, winked his eyes, and exclaimed, "This be a frosty night. 'T is wonderfully cold up North. Ise had a long, cold drive. Uncle John, feel my nose. Is it frozen? My whiskers froze on the way and icicles hung from my eyelids. Ise can hardly see yous." As he stepped to the roaring wood fire and rubbed his hands together, shouts from the children dimmed all other sounds.

"Ise sees my doll sticking out of his pack!"

"That bes my drum, cauz Ise asked for a red drum!"

"No, herns for me, cauz Ise wrote Santa for it!"

When thoroughly warm, Santa walked up the aisle to the loaded tree. The schoolteacher and I handed him the presents from the tree. As Santa called out each name the child came forward for his present. Tiny tots, halfway up to him, turned, fled, and hid in their mother's skirts.

When each child had a toy and had opened a bag of candy

and nuts, the floor resembled a monkey cage in a zoo—shells, cards, paper, and wet dust-laden snow scuffed underfoot. Santa waved farewell, bowed himself out with, "Ise must be mushing on to Whale Head as the children be waiting for me."

Tired sleepy youngsters sucking sticky candy and hugging precious toys were carried back to their homes by their parents.

Christmas Day would be celebrated by as fine a dinner as the housewife could provide—wild duck or goose or rabbit, usually, and raspberry or bagh apple pie, and it would be thoroughly enjoyed; but for the children, at least, the great moment of the festival was the arrival of Santa Claus on Christmas Eve.

From December twentieth to January sixth, mummers, young and old and dressed in outlandish costumes, went from door to door. Just as darkness settled on December twenty-sixth, groups of four, five, or more, gathered in different homes and dressed up. Some wore cardboard cartons with hideous, painted faces and holes cut for eyes, nose, and mouth. Others drew black or colored stockings over their heads and painted eyes and mouths on them. Each mummer draped his body in a sheet, quilt, or gunny sack and carried a stick. Instead of knocking, he thumped on the door, sidled in, sat on the floor, table, or chair and went through grotesque motions. Being a mummer, he was not allowed to speak. If the hostess guessed his name correctly he had to unmask to get his reward of candy or cooky. Many of these mummers dressed every night and went to nearly all the homes in the village. For months mothers who seldom got out during the winter looked forward to mummer time. Grim, grouchy men relaxed and entered wholeheartedly into the sport. It was the best sanity preserver of the year and provided the greatest relaxation and social entertainment.

The firstborn of Mrs. Cragg, the minister's wife, chose to arrive in January, the month when storms and travel are at their worst. Dr. More was asked to come from Harrington Harbour because it promised to be a difficult birth. He left there by dog-team on the thirty-first of December. When halfway there he saw a blizzard rolling in from the sea so he rushed into Whale Head for shelter. For seven days the storm raged and roared, making travel impossible.

At midnight on the seventh the storm's anger reached its peak. At two o'clock I heard Mr. Cragg shouting upstairs for me. He had snowshoed over from the parsonage. I quickly dressed and tied on my snowshoes and left at once with the anxious husband. The bank around the parsonage was more than twenty feet high, soft and wide, so we crouched on our snow-shoes, slid the full length of it, and ended up on the verandah.

I shook the snow from my outer garments, stepped into my uniform, and went upstairs to Mrs. Cragg. This twenty-two-year-old expectant mother had little fear because she had no foreknowledge of what might be ahead of her. Knowing what complications I might have to face alone, I did not look forward with pleasure to what was ahead of me. Experience had taught me that many times the life or death of a baby hung on the nurse doing the right thing at the proper moment.

I told Mr. Cragg that we should have another person who would carry out my instructions without fainting. He did not know of anyone in the harbor on whom he wished to rely, so reluctantly he said, "There is no alternative. I must help you and I will guarantee not to faint."

All night he sat on the top stair just outside our door or paced the hallway, with his head bowed in prayer. My heart ached for him. His mental suffering was almost more agonizing than his wife's physical pain. Each time I opened the door to reassure him that everything was progressing satisfactorily, he jumped to his feet, startled and terrified.

At eight o'clock, I stepped to the door and called, "I need you." Instantly, with a white face, he was at his wife's bedside. I saturated the mask with ether and handed it to him. With an eye on the mask, the clergyman, and the patient, I set to work. Five minutes later, as the cry of a baby girl broke the tenseness, Mr. Cragg dropped the mask, dashed downstairs and out into the fresh air. Heaven never resounded with more thankful prayers than those offered by Mr. Cragg and me.

A NURSE'S life on the Coast is a continual struggle with an almost complete ignorance of modern standards of hygiene.

Although I adhered to the most rigid technique for minor operations and surgical dressings, sterile technique problems were multiple and many times the field was far from sterile. Just as I needed my sterile forceps one grandmother ran her hands over them, exclaiming, "Ise jist wants to make sure yous will'nt burn Dorothy." Another mother stuck her finger into my basin of sterile water "Jist to see that it is not too hot." I explained to her the necessity of keeping everything absolutely sterile and turned to the patient, who asked for a drink. Her mother gave it to her then, before I could stop her, spilled the rest of the drinking water into my sterile basin just as the baby made a quick debut into the world. Bacterial bugs do not present any problem to these people because only bugs seen with the naked eye are considered dangerous.

Most of my babies were delivered under adverse conditions, with semisterile technique, but none of the mothers in our hospital developed any infection. One mother, though, developed mastitis in her home when her baby was six weeks old. I was visiting across the tickle when Mrs. Morrow shouted, "Sister, hern wants to see yous. Hern looks and feels hot and theres a funny, red line on herns breast."

When I arrived Mary was lying on her bed, with a flushed face and a breast swollen twice the normal size. Her temperature was one hundred and two. In a hospital, those borealis rays spreading axilla-ward meant instant action. Operations for such cases require hours of preparation and careful technique. The nearest doctor was travelling the Coast many miles east of us, but something would have to be done. I decided to try external heat and trust to Providence while I went home to read my medical book. Four hours later Mary's temperature had climbed two degrees and I had absorbed all that the medical book could tell me.

At six o'clock that night I proved once more by experience that the good Lord does not expect the impossible and that urgent prayers do not go unheard. On my way to the telegraph office to try to locate the doctor, I saw a dog-team approaching far out on the ice. Before I reached the office, Uncle John shouted, "That be the doctor comin in."

A great weight rolled off my shoulders! As soon as Dr. More arrived and heard the symptoms, without removing his heavy clothing he said, "Let's go right over." We waded a quarter of a mile through knee-deep snow to the Morrow home. Darkness had fallen and because operations by smoking coal oil lamps can prove rather difficult, Dr. More gave Mary a strong sedative and told Mrs. Morrow to have her ready for operation early the next morning. In those days operations were considered "horrible things." Fisherfolk had no confidence in nurses and they *knew* doctors loved to cut people. Gruesome tales were told by patients who had been in the hospital. Most of these tales were invented in order to exaggerate what the patient had gone through and to elicit sympathy. Today the younger generation and many of the older people have quite different opinions. In fact some patients actually have to be turned out of the comfortable hospital beds.

At eight o'clock the next morning, carrying our sterilized equipment, we waded back to the home. Mrs. Morrow greeted us with, "Yous don't need to cut hern. Herns all right and did hern eat a big breakfast!"

Curious to discover what miracle had been wrought, we went inside. Mrs. Morrow continued, "When yous said yous would cut hern, Ise knows hern would die, so Ise got Tom's old, sweaty cap and bound it on hern's breast. By midnight hern began to feel better and hern went to sleep. It's not red. Yous mustn't cut hern."

We examined Mary and most of the redness and inflammation had disappeared. Her temperature was normal, so we did not operate.

I had learned that many of the disorders my patients suffered stemmed from superstition. If a patient had a strong religious faith he had a better chance of recovery. I tried hard to understand the beliefs of these partially illiterate, primitive, superstitious, hard-working folk who live far from public health teaching. Far be it from me to belittle sterile technique, but this miracle case of Mary still puzzles me.

After this experience, I listened to grandmothers. If an onion poultice had cured pneumonia, and there were no other ingredients available for a poultice, it was worth trying. If the child got better, the parents were satisfied and had more confidence in the nurse—for the time at least.

Far back in the woods, Silas Jones got a deep gash in his leg. It was two days before he reached me for first aid treatment. In the woods he remembered that, long before there was a nurse at Mutton Bay, his grandfather had told him about packing cuts with balsam boughs. He packed the bleeding gash with the green balsam branches. The cut had been made with a rusty axe through a greasy, sealskin boot and dirty sock. When I picked out the boughs it was as clean as if it had been cleansed with iodine or peroxide.

Oatmeal poultices give exceptionally good results as substitutes for those made of the conventional linseed. Ocean salt water can replace salicylates for rheumatism. The heat of tobacco smoke relieves earache until some better remedy is obtained. But I drew the line at a mouthful of tobacco juice spat into an infected eye!

As soon as winter had set in everyone began to discuss the possibility of eastern and western trips. At first, this was Greek to me, but soon I learned that it meant the annual winter trip of the doctor or nurse to the people living east or west of the starting place. In summer the visit of the *North Shore* was the fortnightly event. The nurse's eastern trip was the winter event. On these trips the nurse took a miniature dispensary and operating room which included obstetrical and dental equipment. Her drug store contained pills, bandages, dressings, needles, instruments, depressors, applicators, aspirin, and castor oil.

Many homes, inaccessible during the summer, may be visited in winter by dog-team. Lighthouse keepers and whole families spend the summer fishing on bleak islands then move inland in the fall. A winter trip gave the nurse an opportunity to check undernourished babies, haul out rotten teeth, clean up smelly sores, and give mothers pre- and post-natal advice—in fact, to be Jack-of-all-trades in the medical and nursing line.

The latter part of February and early March is the in-between season for fishing, sealing, and wood cutting. The days are longer, the sun warmer, and the trail is well beaten so that travel is much easier. The dogs are well-trained but not too tired from long trips. Seal meat is plentiful so that dogs can be better fed at practically no cost. Sister Martin, it seemed, had been accustomed to make her eastern trip at this time of the year, and I had heard such exciting tales of what happened that I was keenly anticipating one of my own.

Mr. Gray, my driver, did not live in Mutton Bay, so arrangements had to be made several days in advance. On February twentieth, I wrote him to be ready the twenty-eighth. The next morning a reply was brought which read, "Ready any time yous say. I'll be there with lots of dogs."

In my spare time during the next few days, I packed supplies. By the evening of the twenty-seventh, something of everything in my office was packed into a small, wooden travelling box. To supplement native food and for emergencies, nonfreezable food was stored in a separate container. Frozen doughnuts are palatable; cheese never freezes; chocolate bars are nourishing; oatmeal can be cooked quickly to provide heat for cold stomachs; tea is indispensable. Bread, taken from the oven and frozen immediately, is just as fresh when thawed out, and crackers may be eaten without removing mittens. Annie, who was accustomed to packing Sister's food box, made certain that I had a good supply. Later, I realized how invaluable she was, for I would never have thought of half the things she packed.

It was necessary to travel as lightly as possible and, unless something unforeseen happened, I expected to be home in three weeks. We seldom took a complete change of clothing. If I found a spot warm enough to strip to the skin it would be in the combination kitchen-dining room. If it was too warm in a home, I removed one sweater, if too cold, I added one. But there was always the danger of getting soaked to the skin so it was necessary to take several pairs of socks and mitts.

On the afternoon of the twenty-seventh I put in the last minute articles, flashlight, batteries, matches, tooth brush, comb, and reminded by Annie, a good supply of old silk. On long trips cotton or linen handkerchiefs froze stiff and soon chafed one's nose. Paper tissues were useless but silk never froze or chafed.

We expected to start shortly after daylight so I set my alarm clock for six o'clock and went to bed. On long trips a thoroughly heated body at the start meant hours of travel in comfort but a chilled body never really got warm, so I hung my immediate woollens, socks, and skirt over my bedroom chair close to the stovepipe.

But sleep would not come. Troublesome gremlins crept into my mind to keep me awake. First, I had a vision of being snowbound in an isolated spot with no food. Slow freezing from starvation presented a ghastly picture. As that scene faded, I seemed to be trying to deliver a baby but was unable to because I had forgotten my forceps. A suggestion made just before sleep is hard to eradicate. Mole hills grew to mountains. After hours of tossing and turning, I dropped into a non-restful sleep. Immediately, it seemed, I heard someone running up our shed steps, then the kitchen door was flung open. Footsteps ran across the kitchen, down the hall to the foot of the stairs, and an excited, breathless voice shouted up, "Pa hes going. Ma sez don't stop for nothing. Hurry, Sister." Before I could answer, the owner of the voice was out the door and running homeward. Fortunately I knew the voice and where to go.

That morning I learned that death is another event on the Coast which affects young and old and halts all traffic. William White had had a heart attack and by the time I arrived he was drawing his last breath. Everything had happened so quickly that nothing was ready. Usually when death stalks a home, relatives and neighbors take the measurements and have a homemade casket ready.

His wife had a very convenient heart and could collapse when responsibility was asked of her. (Already I had witnessed several convenient non-alarming collapses.) So she flopped on to the couch, raised her hands above her head, and shouted, "I be dying too! Help!"

Her two sons and daughter rushed to her. This added to the general confusion. Since her pulse was strong and regular I could not waste time with her. No doctor or undertaker was available so it was up to me to take charge of these duties. I advised the children to be gentle, sympathetic, but firm with their mother or she would be in hysterics. The eldest son was a huge, awkward lad but had an intelligent mind; I sent him for Uncle John, who knew all the funeral procedure.

Tom returned with Uncle John. The moment he appeared my responsibility as undertaker was ended. In half an hour he was taking the measurements for a casket. Then he went home and returned accompanied by two men, each carrying an armload of narrow boards. By daylight the casket and shell were ready. Uncle John bought black funeral cloth from the local storekeeper. All caskets for adults have to be covered with black cloth. (White flannellette is used for a child.) He stretched this tightly over the wooden casket, tacked it in place, made two wooden handles and bound them with the same material. From left-over scraps, women stitched bands on coat sleeves. Every near relative, including the five-year-old girl, had to wear a black sleeve band.

At ten o'clock Uncle John and the men brought the casket into the front room. We dressed Mr. White in his Sunday suit and placed him in his last earthly resting place. There he reposed until all relatives could arrive, by dog-team, from various harbors.

A death affects the whole village. Previously, when I had been present at deaths, I had called a doctor and undertaker and they did the rest. This time there was no doctor to issue the death certificate, no undertaker to perform the necessary functions, no clergyman to comfort the sorrowing family. A nurse must be prepared to be all of these. Fortunately, the clergyman might be able to reach Mutton Bay for the funeral service. I prayed for fine weather and a clergyman . . . my prayers were answered.

School was dismissed so that all children could attend the funeral. After a simple service six nephews carried the casket over the rocks and lashed it to a komatic. The driver sat on the box in front of the casket and the near relatives climbed onto other dog-teams and followed the so-called hearse. The rest of the men slowly wended their way on foot across the ice. (In summer relatives supply boats for the casket and people.)

Crepe-paper flowers, made by the women, added a bright and cheery touch to the black cloth casket, but contrasted strangely with the white snow and ice.

I could not help comparing this funeral with elaborate city funerals. This was simplicity itself, as are most Coast funerals. Flowers cost a few cents. Flowers and casket cloth were paid for by fish and labor. Relatives made the casket from trees cut in a free wood. They hauled the logs to the mill where the sawmill owner kept half the lumber on a fifty-fifty plan. No money was paid for sawing or preparing. There were no undertaker or doctor's bills. The telegraph operator told the operators of the other harbors. Everyone gave freely of labor and necessary articles because, who knew, perhaps he or she would be the next to need similar help.

Mr. Gray was at the funeral and we arranged to leave on our eastern trip the following Monday—but not until the afternoon. "Ise don't want to interfere," said he, "but yous knows the houses be small and there be only some places wes can stop overnight. It's bestest to start after dinner. Ise knows where we can stop just at dark."

I agreed at once, for there is wisdom in accepting advice from seasoned fishermen.

ONLY a Coast person knows how to tuck the quilts and pillows properly into a coach box to break the wind from all directions. I crawled into my sleeping bag in the coach box and hugged a hot-water bottle while Annie wrapped two blankets about me. As she tucked them leeward and windward, she also tucked into the spare corners small, individually-wrapped packets of food that the heat of my body would keep from freezing. While she worked she kept muttering, "If yous needs just this, all yous has to do is take just this. If yous needs that, take just that." Later, we were extremely grateful for Annie's thoughtful packages. Many times we would have had to remove our mittens and eat our meals with numbed fingers, had all the food been in one packet.

At two o'clock Mr. Gray spread his heavy deerskin over the drug box and climbed onto it. I scrambled up behind him. The dogs were straining at the traces and yapping to be away. Mr. Gray hauled up the chain drags from under the front komatic runners, snapped his snake whip, Annie clicked the camera, the crowd shouted, "Lucky trip!" "Come back!" "Mind the open water," and we were off.

The dogs clawed their way up the steep rocks. Soon we dropped over the top of the cliff and the Station was lost from view. This time, unless a telegram awaited me at the next village, we were really on our eastern trip. I drew a sigh of relief, settled into the cozy blankets, and entered into the spirit of the adventure.

We shot down the trail on the west side of the precipice and out onto the open bay. Mr. Gray shouted back, "Wes on Red Bay trail." It was nearly suppertime when the dogs bolted down a steep hill and halted before a fisherman's home. "Wes'll stop overnight here at La Tabatierre and start at dawn tomorrow. The Lord willing and the weather permitting, wes'll make St. Augustine tomorrow night. Wes'll pass Shekatika Bay but there be no room for us to sleep there."

From mouth to mouth, news travels sixty miles an hour. When we arrived at Mrs. Robert's door at six o'clock, she was expecting us. The tempting odor of a steaming seal pie and hot biscuits greeted us. As we ate the good food, new energy coursed through our chilled bodies.

Several times during January and February I had been called

to this village, so there was not much work to do that night. The next morning at five-thirty I was wakened by Mrs. Robert calling through the bedroom door. "Mr. Gray hes wants to get away. Your breakfast be ready." We ate our boiled salt herring and at six o'clock, while the light was still dusky, we were off again. Soon far out on the ice the sun spread rays of flashing silver all about us as they penetrated the overhanging clouds. Nothing but dazzling whiteness, ice, and snow could be seen. An amazing sense of direction carried Mr. Gray unerringly across the desert of ice.

We mushed and snaked our way through the underbrush on the narrow trail over a portage. The radiant sparkle of the sun on the snow-laden branches far surpassed in beauty any artificially lighted Christmas tree.

At noon we catapulted down a steep cliff and the speed of the dogs started the komatic up the next hill, which towered above us. The dogs clawed and dug their toenails into the ice and seemed to climb straight up in the air. Eventually the leader dog went over the top of the cliff, then the next and next, until the last dog had his front paws safely over the ridge. Apparently they forgot that I was behind in the coach box, helplessly swathed in blankets, for with a bound they cleared the top. This was too much for the komatic, suspended partially over the brim of the precipice. Before I had time to think, it capsized.

Blankets, thermos bottle, camera, food, hot-water bottle, and I tumbled from the komatic and, like snowballs gathering momentum, we rolled and spun back to the bottom of the hill. There was not a ridge or crevice on that icy surface to gain a foothold. Like Winnie the Pooh, plunk, I landed in a deep snowbank at the bottom of the hill.

Halfway up the cliff, Mr. Gray clung to the crust and shouted down, "Are yous there?" For some reason this tickled my funny bone and I burst out laughing. Where did he think I would be? But my mirth was momentary. There was real consternation in his voice. So I shouted up, "Sure, it was a grand slide." He crawled to a sitting position, folded his arms across his chest, put both sealskin-booted legs close together like skis, and came skidding, like a log shot from a chute, down to where I was buried in the snow. Together we gathered up the scattered pieces. The only damage was a hole pierced in my camera bellows. My irreplaceable snapshots were lost. My camera would have to be sent to Toronto, and would not be returned before June so my supply of films was useless. All those wonderful snapshots I had hoped to take home with me were a dream of the past. I decided to make mental pictures so that later I might be able to depict some of them in writing.

We dug our toes and fingers into the crust and slowly inched our way to the top. It was one o'clock and we were tired and hungry so we decided to have our lunch. A Coast outdoor meal is never complete without strong boiled tea, on the top of which float a few twigs and ashes. Mr. Gray gathered dead boughs and scooped out a hole in the snow beside a sheltered rock. He hung his wire-handled, tin can teapot on a green stick over the flames and in no time his black tea was boiling. He drank three cups but I refrained from indulging in such a concoction. Refreshed by frozen doughnuts, cheese, crackers, and chocolate bars, we collected our dogs and started off again.

Leaving the next portage trail, we came to an open glade. Here the new trail passed within a few inches of treacherous rapids. Every moment I expected to see one of the dogs lose his foothold and drag all of us down with him. The open glade ran, like a jagged scar, through the white and blue of snow and ice. A transparent skin of ice reached out from the edge as if striving to heal the gaping wound. I had a vivid picture of being swiftly drawn under the ice and as swiftly disappearing, like the floating crust, beneath the surface, so I shouted to Mr. Gray, "Shall I walk and lessen the load?" I hoped he would not accept my offer for green sealskin boots have a habit of slipping suddenly from under one at an unexpected moment. He shouted back, "Sister, don't yous dare move. Hold tight to the komatic and sit still. Wes all right." I obeyed his commands and we reached the other side safely.

Scarcely had we passed this gaping glade when we approached another. When in dangerous places, fishermen like to tell gruesome stories to Off-coasters to see if they can make their hair stand on end. I will not vouch for the truth of this tale Mr. Gray entertained me with. "Right here be the place where Mrs. Manly fell headlong off the back of the komatic and was sucked under. Just like that." He snapped his fingers to illustrate the quickness of her disappearance. "Hern was never seen again. It all happened like this. Hern's son-in-law was the driver. Theyse never did hit it off together. Hern led him a merry life. Just as they were passing this spot, suddenly, as if the very devil were after them, the dogs bolted. The quickness caught her off guard and threw hern backwards into the rapids." As an afterthought, he chuckled and added, "Some say this is not true and that the son-in-law suddenly lashed his whip to make the dogs take that unexpected spurt. God rest hern's soul. The family lived happily ever after."

Shut in by impenetrable high, rocky cliffs we mushed over the ice. There were no homes to be seen and I could not distinguish any landmark. Suddenly Mr. Gray halted the dogs, stepped off the komatic, scratched his head, looked about, and exclaimed, "Well, Ise'll be jiggered. Ise would've sworn Ise knews every inch of these banks, but Ise'll admit wes lost. Somewhere, Ise missed the trail where wes should've left through the opening in the rocks."

He threw the steel chain drags under the front komatic runners to stop the dogs and said gravely, "Yous mustn't leave the komatic. If yous removes your weight from it the dogs will dash for home. Wes would be in a nice mess out here on the ice with night settling in. Should theyse attempt to go, yous must stand all yous weight on the runners so that the drags will cut into the ice."

With this warning he went in search of an opening in the rocks. The sameness everywhere would so bewilder a stranger that he could be lost in a few moments. This thought must have flashed through Mr. Gray's mind because, when he had gone five hundred yards, he shouted back, "Don't under any condition step off the komatic. Ise'll be back in a few minutes."

Though I had been out on the open ice since six o'clock that morning, and much as I would have appreciated stepping off, I intended to stick closer to that komatic than the bark clings to a tree. A night on the open ice did not appeal to me.

Mr. Gray, confident that the opening was there, searched each side of the shore. The wind grew more chilly and biting. Twilight came and I could not see any living thing except those fretting dogs on which my life depended. Finally, from far across the ice came a faint, but cheery, "Hullo," which I answered. Then out of the darkness came a welcome figure. Mr.

Gray had not been far off in his instinctive calculations because half a mile down the river we had passed the opening. He jumped on the komatic, turned the dogs around and headed back. Soon we were leaving the ice through that opening. As the dogs took the upward climb, Mr. Gray turned and remarked, "If yous wish to stretch your legs, Ise'll wait for yous over the top of the cliff." This was a welcome release. I extricated myself from my sleeping bag, stumbled out of the coach box, and lagged behind. At the top he was waiting for me. Cramped muscles functioned once more and all chilliness was gone, so I wiggled into the sleeping bag and we mushed on our way.

By now it was too dusky to distinguish objects three feet from us. Every few moments, thinking I must be frightened, Mr. Gray called back, "Soon wes'll be there. Wes cannot get lost as wes are following the telegraph poles, they'se spotted (blazed)." Now I knew how he had been able to locate the opening in the rocks. Reassured that sooner or later we would emerge once more, I began to speculate as to what would await us at the end of the trail.

"Ah!" exclaimed Mr. Gray at long last, satisfaction in his voice. "This be the hill!"

He shouted to the dogs and they halted instantly on the very brink of one of the steepest hills I have ever seen. He stepped off the komatic, again scratched his head and meditated for a few seconds, then said, "Sister, Ise figger the bestest way to avoid a crash is to unhitch the dogs and usn'll walk down." I agreed that the safest way was to unhitch the dogs but I was not convinced about the safety of walking down that perpendicular cliff. But there was no other way. As I gazed down the hill I decided I would never attempt to walk down. My boots were made of untanned sealskin, known as "green sealskin," scraped and dried until waterproof. They were not designed for negotiating cliffs like this. Fortunately, under my heavy woollen skirt, my thick drill breeches had reinforced seats. I jumped off.

As soon as Mr. Gray unhitched the dogs they bounded, yapping, down the hill. With the toe of his boot he kicked the komatic and it shot straight as an arrow down the cliff and stopped far out on the ice.

"Now wes goes," he exclaimed.

Side by side, we sat down, but unlike the komatic with its steel shoes, we struck every frozen hubble as we slid down. Some of these lumps loosened and travelled with us. Others stubbornly resisted, leaving us with huge black-blue welts. Seat sore, at last we reached the komatic.

The dogs had satisfied their thirst by lapping snow and refreshed themselves by rolling in the drifts and now were yapping to be away. They frisked about and tried to evade us but we finally managed to catch the ends of their traces. Mr. Gray slipped all the loops over the komatic pit rope, untangled the traces, and we were off across the bay.

Half an hour later we mushed around a jutting point where a weather-beaten, dilapidated shack jumped at us from the cove. It was the Marconi operator's house. Sheltered from the worst winds, the only home in this part of the Coast, Mr. Peters' house was an oasis in the desert. Outside, here and there, spikes of black hair stuck through the top of mounds of freshly fallen snow that looked like little igloos. Underneath these mounds several exhausted black dogs were asleep with their hair sprouting through the top. Unlike most dogs, they did not budge at the approach of a strange team, but remained curled up in their snow nests.

As I groped about in the darkness for the outer latch the door opened and Coast hospitality greeted me. What a relief and comfort to find shelter in the warmth of such a friendly home! And our hosts made us feel that it was a treat to have visitors—as indeed it was, for few travellers passed this way.

The kerosene lamp strung from the low ceiling threw a golden glow about the kitchen. Inside the house, bare of comforts, difficult to warm, destitute of luxury, the people lived their quiet life, feared no dangers, accepted adversity as part of their daily routine, welcomed strangers as long-lost relatives, and shared with them their best.

Now I knew why the dogs outside were too tired to utter their customary howling welcome. Sitting by the roaring kitchen fire were Mr. Cragg and his driver. They had arrived from the east an hour before and had sought shelter for the night.

As a rule winter homes are compact and crowded to capacity. This home, too small to house its own brood of five, would have to stretch to accommodate four more. But Coast hospitality is never limited; everyone is welcome to the best the hostess can afford, and here was no exception.

Mr. Cragg had come from St. Paul's River, where overnight an epidemic of flu had struck the village. Word had been sent by him to ask me to rush to them as fast as possible. We would have to change our plans and leave the in-between villages until our homeward trip.

Difficulties confronted us at nine o'clock. Rather embarrassed, Mrs. Peters whispered to me, "Ise sorry, but wes has only one guest bedroom and Ise wants it for Mr. Cragg. You will have my bed. Would yous go to bed now and pass out the lamp so Mr. Cragg may have it? Wes only has one lamp." The family went to bed in the dark.

I crawled into a narrow, homemade bunk behind a blue checked gingham curtain, stretched my weary limbs between two quilts spread over some hay which padded the board slats, and passed the lamp out to Mrs. Peters. Shortly afterward, on the other side of the curtain, Mrs. Peters and her brood burrowed under the quilts in the other bunk. In a few moments the sound of snoring informed me that they were sound asleep. Mr. Cragg had a cozy, soft, goose-feather tick. The drivers and the father and eldest boy curled up on blankets on the hard kitchen floor and probably slept well—better than I did.

The next morning I examined the children and counselled and advised the parents. After a boiled salt herring breakfast we carried our blankets out to the coach box. When I wiggled into my sleeping bag, painful twinges reminded me of our recent bumpy slide.

At three o'clock in the afternoon a dog-team drew alongside of us. It was Mr. Cragg and his driver. Just after we had left, he said, word came over the wire that a little lad had fallen through the ice, had had a convulsion, and apparently lay dying from pneumonia. The wire stated that he was gasping for breath and the parents wanted a clergyman and nurse to rush to him.

When we reached the home little Paul was chasing his brother around the table. Coast people often act first and think afterward. Dodds' Almanac said pneumonia followed convulsions and was fatal. Mrs. Teal *knew* he would have pneumonia because he was in convulsions. Paul had indiscreetly eaten too much fresh seal meat. When nature upheaved the contents of his stomach the convulsion ceased.

It was too late to attempt to reach St. Paul's River that night, so we must spend another night in very crowded quarters.

At six o'clock the next day the student clergyman, Mr. Morel, and his housekeeper welcomed us at the parsonage of St. Paul's River.

After a hot partridge supper, Mr. Morel and I started to visit the sick. Seventy-five men, women, and children were in bed, huddled over stoves, lying on couches or curled up on the floor beside the hot stoves. As I went from home to home examining, diagnosing, and treating, it was difficult to decide which ones should receive my limited amount of drugs. The older people, who could take them, would not remain in bed. The middle-aged insisted that they could not stay in bed because they had to stoke fires and look after the sick and the babies. It was dangerous to give pills for the small babies. My drugs were too precious to be handed out indiscreetly. Since I had to be home at a certain time for a maternity case and did not have half enough drugs for this village, I wired the doctor. He agreed that this was an urgent situation and said he would start the next day. He advised me, unless I heard from him, to be ready to start home on a definite day so that we would not expect accommodation at the same place, yet we would not leave the village alone overnight. This was one time I longed to be three nurses—one here, one en route, and one at Mutton Bay.

For a week, from early morning until far into the night, I went from one patient to another, easing a gasping baby, softening and freshening the pillows of men and women, holding cups of water and dropping pills into mouths of patients whose hearts raced so fast they could not hold the cup steady, preparing gargles for kinkorns that would not glutch. ("Kinkorn" is the local term for Adam's apple. When one has a sore throat and tries to swallow, his "kinkorn will not glutch.")

In such a short time and with so many patients I could do very little, though the need was great. The last morning, with a sad heart, I visited each home and left instructions to be followed until the doctor arrived. I knew it would be the survival of the fittest. Afterward I learned that only four elderly persons, who would not remain in bed, died, but years later treatment was given to dozens who suffered from direct or indirect results of this epidemic.

At noon we drew up alongside Dr. John's dog-team, where I replenished my drug kit so that I could visit the in-between villages.

Two nights later we reached St. Augustine. Here, I learned again that a nurse has to be Jack-of-all-trades. When spending three years training to be a nurse I did not think that one day my duties would include making dog shoes!

For two days we had travelled from early morning until dark over soft ice covered with a thin crust of salt slob. The crust and slob had cut the dogs' paws until they were bleeding at every step. It would be cruel to make them travel for a day or two.

The wife of the Hudson's Bay clerk, Mrs. Cameron, invited us to spend two days with them while the paws healed. We purchased some heavy canvas in their store and Mrs. Cameron patiently showed me how to make dog shoes. Eight dogs, with four paws each, had to be shod. Allowing for extras we cut forty shoes. These shoes are made from a piece of canvas eight inches long and three inches wide. We folded it in the center so that there would not be any seam under the paws, then I stitched up each side and finished with a drawstring around the top. When this shoe is pulled over a dog's paw it resembles a baby's thumbless mitt.

At last we were ready to start again. By eerie lamplight we ate our steaming oatmeal and bread and butter and drank strong coffee, shod our dogs, and in the cold frosty darkness started homeward. The semihealed paws, protected by canvas, seemed hardly to feel the crust and slob; rested and headed for home, the dogs travelled twice as fast as before. Frequently one of the shoes would slip off, but seldom did the driver lose one. As the komatic swept along behind the dogs, Mr. Gray, with a long, quick swoop, snatched the shoe from the ice. When we reached a convenient stopping place, he halted the team, reshoed, and checked the paws. Occasionally he shouted back, "Dog shoe," and I, knowing he had seen a shoe on the ice but had missed catching it, would grab for it. If I missed it he stopped the dogs and I ran back while he waited for me.

By ten o'clock we came to the bush trail and it was evident that somewhere, somehow, Mr. Gray had imbibed something stronger than coffee. Normally he was a most careful driver. He knew every inch of the Coast and when and where to take chances. But now, on steep hills where usually two drags were used, he never slackened the pace of the dogs. Without applying any drags, we whizzed down at full speed. Recklessly, he urged the dogs to a breakneck speed. We rushed down hills, bolted and swerved round stumps and "ballacaters"—huge salt ice balls formed by the sea washing against cakes of loose ice until a ball is formed. Had the komatic run onto the dogs they would have been instantly killed. Had we been thrown nothing would have saved us.

When we reached a safe spot I recalled how food sobered intoxicated patients so I suggested that we stop for lunch. The hot tea, with its floating cinders, cleared Mr. Gray's brain and for the rest of the day he was extremely cautious, courteous, and full of apologies.

During the next few days we stopped in villages and I peered at mushroom tonsils, examined running pink eyes, cleaned sores, and syringed ears.

When our dogs arrived at the Station, I joyfully edged my cramped, creaking joints out of the sleeping bag. Annie came running out to welcome me. My eastern trip had been both exciting and, I hoped, useful. Now how good it was to be home again!

TODAY a complicated problem had to be solved. A wire came from the doctor stating, "Doctor and wife on way." Doctors and their wives are not fond of being crowded into small wards with crying babies. A maternity patient with a seven-day-old baby occupied our only spare bed. To get her home we would have to cross a quarter of a mile of glare ice. The first fisherman shook his head. "Nothing doing, no dogs can keep their feet on this ice," he said. In front of the next house several dogs were curled, blocking the only path. I stepped safely over the first dog but, just as I raised my foot to clear the next with a quick leap, he sent me sprawling into a snowbank. Amused at my undignified approach, the next man said with a laugh, "How do yous expect dogs to keep their feet when the nurse can't?" Another shook his head and muttered, "No use trying, ice is ice wherever it is." In despair I gave up and went home to think.

Before I reached the Station a brain wave halted me. Would it be possible to use men for dog power? I went back to the men and asked them. "Sure, Sister," one of them replied, "wes can do that. Ise thought of it when yous suggested dogs, but yous never did ask me."

Soon four men were hitched to the komatic. With a wink to the other men, Uncle John, still chuckling over my spill, said, "Yous can't keep your feet on ice any better than dogs. Jump into the coach box and we will draw all of yous in one trip."

I did not argue. With the baby in my arms I crawled into the box. The komatic skidded and slewed. The lead man took a step forward but his sealskin boots shot from underneath him. But, in a second, unhurt, he was up hauling his part of the load. We reached the other side of the tickle safely and I tucked the mother and baby into their own bed.

A quick shift changed the ward into a comfortable guest room for the doctor and his wife.

On the eighth of May I had my last komatic ride for the season, an unexpected one. Mr. Cragg was visiting inland when his wife, overcome by a wave of homesickness, decided she wanted to send a telegram home. The telegraph office was six miles away so she came over and begged me to go with her. I knew it was not the right thing to do, but she coaxed so hard that I finally yielded. Neither of us had ever driven a dog-team without a driver along. But Providence was with us and took us safely to the office.

Mrs. Cragg sent her message and went out to the dog-team to start home. When leaving dogs hitched to a komatic, the men always turn it bottomside up and dig the front runners into the snow. We had done this. Now we turned the komatic right side up and Mrs. Cragg jumped on. As I jumped I caught one foot in a dog trace which sent me head first into the snowbank. Mrs. Cragg looked back to see if I were hurt. Just as she turned, the dogs swerved around a ballacater and spilled her off the other side. Then finding themselves free, they headed for home. Fortunately, a hundred feet ahead, the second dog ran onto another ballacater. This brought the whole team to a dead stop and saved the day.

We shouted back to the Roberts family begging them never to tell Mr. Cragg about our mishap. Once more we clung to the komatic and headed homeward, thankful that we did not have to hike six miles through icy slob water and congratulating ourselves that in an emergency we could handle a dog-team.

But "Pride goeth before a fall." Half a mile from home a dog-team swiftly approached us and when it drew alongside, we recognized Mr. Cragg. His facial expression left no doubt as to his feelings. He had evidently been much worried about our safety and now that he found us unharmed must have felt vexed, for he hardly exchanged a word with us as he turned his team around and accompanied us home.

Each time I dipped up a glass of water from our bucket, several tiny, wiggling specks darted across the bottom of the dipper. This was a sure sign of spring.

Our reservoir was a pond up on the hill, and the winter trail for dogs and pedestrians crossed its full length. Every day throughout the winter, village teams drove up, cut holes in the ice, and drew down barrels of water. Now the ice and snow had started to melt on this much-traversed thoroughfare and all sorts of things floated in our drinking water barrel. Wigglers, bugs, and leaves soon formed a squirming mass at the bottom.

During part of the summer we had dipped our drinking water from a pond back of the Station which was fed from the hills above. Now I decided, if possible, to shovel off a few feet of snow and cut through the ice to this source. Carrying a shovel, axe, pail, and dipper, Annie and I plodded up the hill. We shovelled and cut until finally we were rewarded by seeing the tempting water through a hole large enough to put the dipper through. How were we to reach it? I decided to take the plunge.

I weighed one hundred and forty pounds while Annie weighed only a hundred, but she was wiry and strong. She grasped my feet firmly in both hands and carefully I slid my body over the brim and painfully edged downward, pushing the pail and dipper ahead of me. It was deeper than I had foreseen. As I felt my head going miles down and my feet waving perpendicularly, I shouted up, "Don't let go or I will smother." Faintly, miles away, I heard, "Ise'll hold yous."

Finally the dipper plopped against icy water and laboriously, a cupful at a time, I dipped the precious liquid into my small pail. When it was half full and the blood in my temples felt ready to burst, I shouted, "Pull." Annie tugged and I inched, feet first, upward.

We had our first long drink of clear, icy cold water since the previous fall.

But I did not intend to be a daily bucket dangler at the end of an human windlass. Eventually we rigged up a wire-string-pail-water-windlass which solved our drinking problem until late spring when the freshet washed away the bulk of winter refuse so that we could use our pond reservoir. Of course we always knew that whenever the dogs felt hot they enjoyed a swim, and perhaps that swim had been taken in our reservoir after they had been gorging on decayed cod heads!

With spring came the excitement of mail. It had been accumulating through the fall and winter, and it might contain many surprises. The local mailman might bring mail and parcels dated back to September or October that had missed the fall boat, anything left at anytime during the winter, or mail left by mistake at some other harbor between October and May.

Late on the afternoon of May twenty-second a snow squall ceased and faintly we could hear the familiar hum of John's small boat. One by one, until we were thirty men and women, we straggled to the church steps where we could get the first view. Cautiously he snaked his way amid treacherous ice floes and we could hear the chug of his motor more distinctly until finally we saw a dark speck moving among the greenish-white floes. At times we would lose sight of the speck, then it would reappear a hundred feet nearer. Before John was halfway into the wharf, nearly the whole village had gathered at the shore. When his mail boat thumped the wharf, we swarmed about it. He flung the mailbags onto the rocks and waiting men grabbed them and ran with them to the post office where volunteers eagerly helped the postmistress sort and distribute the mail.

At nine o'clock that night the last letter was handed through the wicket. I received seven personal letters, twelve business ones, five magazines, six parcels, and thirty daily papers, ranging from January to May. Night was turned into day. At two o'clock in the morning most of my letters were digested and I was again in contact with an outside world.

Two weeks later men and women rushed from house to house shouting, "Herns left Harrington!" "Herns must be nearing here!" "Herns" was the *North Shore*, steaming toward Mutton Bay on her first spring trip. Our fall "fresh" supplies could hardly be called fresh now so this boat was welcomed with open arms. Watching for icebergs, she steamed her way inward among the ice pans. Jim sighted her first and shouted, "Herns turning in!" Suddenly, we saw her slowly turning back. Our hearts sank. Shouts from dry throats echoed across the water.

"Wes'll starve."

"Ise no more flour."

"Ise put my last cup of flour in the oven this morning."

"Ise only tea and fish left."

Jim turned to Uncle John and pleaded, "Can yous spare usn a little lard and tea if hern don't make it? Ise don't minds so much for myself but it's hard to see the younguns munching dry bread."

And then joyful shouts rang out.

"Herns swinging around!"

"Look, herns past that green floe."

"Ise bet hern'll make it!"

The excitement grew and grew. Unable to hold the children's attention, the teacher dismissed classes. We scrambled aboard Uncle John's boat and as soon as the steamer cast anchor we swarmed up the sailor's ladder and raided the steward's store.

With arms full of oranges, grapefruit, cucumbers, and ginger ale, we plied the officers with questions.

"When will the rest of the supplies get through?"

"Will drift ice block the harbor again or has navigation really started?"

"What is going on outside?"

They, in turn, queried us.

"Did you have a good winter?"

"Seen any seals yet?"

"Much snow? Many deaths?"

Good-natured Captain Legault, seeing that we could not all get down the ladder with our arms full of fruit, ordered the sailors to lower us to our boats in his crane freight net-basket. Slowly we creaked out over the deck, cleared the rail, then hung, a basket of human cargo, suspended midway between heaven and earth. Then down, down, far out over the icy water we swung, until we stood upright over our boat. Uncle John unhooked the snap and we stepped out of the basket.

That night, like Eskimos after a whale catch, we gorged on fresh fruit and dreamed of steamer mail to come.

"Mum said to wait for an answer."

That is all I heard of Bertha's conversation with Annie. It was a balmy June morning. I was eating an early breakfast when Annie came to the dining room and handed me the telegram from the doctor in Harrington asking, "Can you come at once? Our nurse too sick to work. If no patients in ward close Station."

We were in the midst of housecleaning but that was a secondary matter and could wait. As usual when leaving the Station, we had to dole laxatives, aspirins, toothache drops, and gargles to the neighboring homes, just in case. For the Station was the only dispensary and when the nurse left there were no drugs available.

When I returned from my round of visits I saw Uncle Ed and Bob tying the Mission boat at our wharf. Before we reached the Station one of those sudden nor'wester growlers howled across the tickle, bringing heavy pelting rain with it. Uncle Ed scanned the eastern, western, northern, and southern skies and then walked over to Uncle John and Uncle Ted. They put their heads together and all agreed that we should reach Harrington some time that night. All signs, they said, portended a worse day on the morrow. Annie and I rustled up a hurry-up lunch, then started encasing ourselves in woollens and rainproof clothing while Uncle Ed and Bob washed the dishes. Even in the face of a storm, it would never do to leave unwashed dishes. I had spent too many months training maids that dishes must not be left to coax flies and mice.

Tiny, squirrel-agile, chirping, weather-worn Uncle Ed, with his keen sense of humor and chivalry, always thought of the comforts of others; he was the doctor's right-hand man. Faithful as a Coast dog that will die at the post rather than desert his master in time of trouble, he went out and brought the boat close to the Mission rocks. Unfortunately the doctor had sent the open boat and not the comfortable Mission boat in which he usually travelled. This meant a biting cold, wet trip. By the time we reached the wharf, water streamed from our sou'westers and slickers. White caps scudded across the waves and far out at sea we could hear the breakers booming against the rocks. Spray flew high and rain drenched everything. As we picked our way between shoals and islands, scanning each breaker for treacherous, hidden reefs, we could hear the thundering roar of the sea. Here and there we caught a glimpse of a huge grampus jumping out of the water. Soon salt-water rivulets trickled from my face. These rivulets tasted like the ocean and emitted that briny odor so closely associated with seasickness. The swaying motion of the sea did not help matters. Green and limp, I collapsed against the side of the boat. Uncle Ed shouted above the thunderous roar of the sea.

"It be a spell of weather. Hope we reach Harrington tonight. There'll be no travel tomorrow. Keep this canvas well around yous. The wind eats to the marrow."

The sea grew rougher, the breakers roared louder, the air grew colder, and the spume tasted saltier. The boat pitched and tossed from side to side. No longer able to sit on the seat, I clung to Uncle Ed's leg while he braced himself at the steering rudder. As always, Uncle Ed's calm, confident manner and wrinkled, cheerful face gave me moral support. He placed a board above my head to protect me from the extreme force of the gale. But this only added to my discomfort because it acted as an eave spout, directing the cold trickle down my already gooseflesh neck.

The force of each wave made the boat shudder as vast convulsions shook it from stem to stern. By four o'clock it was rolling hideously and darkness settled about us. Nothing could be seen across the great black expanse except imaginary shapes like phantom specters along the shore. Through and around these ghostly figures the wind made curious wailing sounds. Not a star could be seen in the ink-black sky; not a gleam of light shone from the shore; all about was blackness and the booming of the sea. The even rhythm of the great piston engines was broken by pulsating throbs. As the boat pitched into a breaker it would miss a beat, pick up the lost pulse, and roll back to the next wave.

Suddenly, out of the darkness in front of us, a light flickered, then another. Hope revived. Soon cold and wetness would be forgotten beside the Mission fire.

Tiny specks of twinkling and flickering lights appeared in cottage windows. Far ahead, faintly, we could distinguish the friendly beacon light. A monstrous wave pitched us around the point; out of the darkness and rain came a voice, and then undistinguishable figures moved about. The doctor's friendly voice shouted down, "Heave to! Pull her in!" followed by, "Mind your step. It is wonderful slippery." Through the rays of his flashlight, I could dimly see his arm reaching down. I grabbed his hand, he hauled, and I heaved myself to the slippery stage.

In a surprised but pleased voice, the doctor exclaimed, "I did not expect you would make it tonight. It's a mighty rough sea."

An Off-coaster can never understand the joys and warmth that await one after such a trip. While supper was being prepared, we toasted ourselves before a roaring fire, then consumed huge quantities of steaming fresh fish, homemade biscuits, and redberries.

Sick as she was, Miss Flarry was able to give me her report before she crawled into bed and I went on night duty. It was a difficult night. I had already endured twelve strenuous hours and the storm followed me into the hospital. The wind howled through doors and windows, rain trickled through the ceiling to the rubber sheets on the porch beds. Outside, the rain came down in torrents and huge breakers crashed against the rocks;

amid all this noise, bells rang and I searched for the owners in an unfamiliar hospital.

Night ended at last and dawn broke what seemed almost a nightmare. After breakfast the doctor agreed that, since I had to go on night duty again, it would be best for me to go to bed for a few hours before scrubbing for operations. At noon, after several years of non-practice, I donned a sterile gown and gloves and assisted the doctor.

Operating on the Coast was not quite as simple, or shall I say it was more simple, than in a city hospital staffed with trained, efficient doctors, nurses, orderlies, and assistants. Hot and cold water did not gush from a tap. We had to pump the water to the kitchen, heat it on the stove and carry it upstairs to the make-shift operating room. Coal oil lamps and flashlights had to be placed in position so that, in an emergency, they could be turned on instantly. I showed Mary, the maid, how to circulate for us, then I started the anæsthetic while the doctor scrubbed. This was new work for me; I had to watch the patient to note any change in pulse and breathing, keep an eye on Mary to prevent her contaminating our sterile field, and at the same time take care of the doctor's needs. When he was ready he watched the patient while I scrubbed. She made a splendid recovery and, fourteen years later, she asked me if I remembered my first Coast operation. As if I could ever forget it!

After three operations, I went back to bed for a couple of hours before going on night duty. The next three days were nightmares of nursing, issuing clothing, spreading redberries on the rocks, bathing babies, and supervising maids. Between spells I caught a few winks of sleep at night, with an ear open for bells and babies demanding night feedings. At the end of the week

Miss Flarry was able to reassume her duties and I was free to return to my Station.

On the Coast the familiar slogans are, "The Lord willing," "The weather permitting," and "No hurry, no worry." I had to content myself with these now as I began a typical Coast wait.

The hourly, daily, and yearly test of patience practised by fisherfolk who wait on weather and sea is marvellous to behold, especially in these days of restless, changing, and unsettled humanity. For them a day's wait may mean starvation before spring yet, when a gale rages, although traps and nets may be washed away and with them hundreds of dollars, they patiently wait. Fish may break from nets and most of the winter's food be lost, but the fisherman sits and waits, optimistically hoping and deep down in his heart uttering a prayer that all will be well. Without grumbling or complaining, he watches the sky and wonders what he will find when eventually the gale ceases and he is able to go to his nets.

At noon a boy came with a note saying, "Too rough. Ise'll not go today. Ise'll be up after dinner to discuss tomorrow." At four o'clock, Jack, the mailman, came. He inspected the barometer, felt the air, studied the sea, and, out of courtesy, sought the doctor's advice.

Sunday morning the boy returned with another note saying, "Going soon." In an hour Jack came around the point with his mail boat. A drizzling rain soon made everything slippery, soggy, and clammy. Chilled to the marrow and with a hard mailbag for a pillow, I succumbed to the pangs of seasickness. As I leaned weakly over the edge of the boat I wondered whether or not it was all worth while.

For those who have never had the privilege of travelling on a Coast mail boat, I would say that its atmosphere is friendly, even chummy. Everyone is soon interested in everyone else and enquires where he is going, what is his business, and how long he is going to stay.

In these small boats one may find Mission workers, traders, priests, fishermen and their families crowded together in happy camaraderie. Barrels, boxes, guns, baby bundles, canned food, babies, and slop pails are huddled together. One, two, or three persons curl up on a six-foot berth, on the floor, or on benches along the wall with a mailbag or a parcel for a pillow. The cabin gets stifling hot, reeks with perspiration, tobacco, feet, sealskin boots, gasoline, dog harnesses, and seasick odors. But every mailman goes prepared for emergencies. A grey enamel basin hangs in a handy place. When the first rush of seasickness sweeps over one of the passengers, everyone jumps to assist him. Someone grabs the basin and passes it over. Practically all sympathize because they too have required this emergency basin sometime or other.

Meals are called "mug-ups" and consist of anything at any time—chiefly boiled black tea and a hunk of bread with a thick layer of lard or butter. But each meal is a social occasion. With two-inch slices of bread and lard in one hand, and a heavy, chipped granite mug of strong tea in the other, swaying to the rhythm of the boat, everyone chats about fish, sea, and weather.

Today travelling conditions have somewhat improved. Mail boats are larger and have cabins big enough to accommodate many passengers. I have travelled on them under adverse conditions, but always the mailman showed that thoughtfulness and courtesy known only to one accustomed to humanity in times of great need.

At four o'clock in the afternoon, wreaths of clouds that rode like smoke scudded across the sky, warning us that a dark night was ahead. Slowly we crept through the darkness to our wharf where two boys were waiting to take my bags. They half dragged me as I stumbled up the slippery stage over greasy rocks to the Station. Once again I was happy to be home and knew how worth while it was to be living and working with these friendly, kind folk.

The Station was cold, so Fred set my bags in the kitchen, went to the shed, brought in wood, and made a roaring fire. I bade him a cordial good night and without waiting to remove my woollens tucked myself into bed with a hot-water bottle at my feet and slept like a newborn babe.

WILL arrive Mutton Bay tomorrow afternoon. Bringing Bishop. Get church ready. Bring down Bishop's chair."

Details as to where I would find this important chair and where to put it were included in the telegram, which came from Mr. Cragg.

Mrs. Cragg was away on holidays and she had left the parsonage key with me so that I could water her plants.

Never before had I entertained a bishop, but many times Mr. Cragg had come to my assistance in an emergency so I must not let him down. Should the chair be in the wrong spot, kneeling pads in improper places, or the wrong altar cloth on the table, someone in the congregation would spot it before the service started. But what could a bishop who came only every four years expect?

Anyone wishing to be confirmed during the next four years must be ready tomorrow night. Like a colony of disrupted ants the people darted to and fro. Clothing had to be pressed, dresses and suits lengthened or shortened while the pros and cons for and against those who were candidates for confirmation were discussed.

Mrs. Moss came to ask me if I thought John would look ridiculous with the legs and sleeves of his suit too short for his fast-growing limbs. Should he wait four years? Life was so uncertain on the Coast. It would be a tragedy for him to die unconfirmed. I assured her that I was certain the good Lord would excuse short sleeves but He might not excuse a four-year wait because of vanity.

Mrs. Thes rushed over to know if May's dress was long enough. Or should she let down the hem and take a chance on the faded demarcation line being too conspicuous?

Borrowing, letting down, hemming, and dressmaking went on all afternoon and far into the night.

Next day we unlocked the parsonage, hauled down the Bishop's heavy chair, and placed it in position by the altar. Women and girls set to work with brooms and cloths to raise clouds of dust as they cleaned the church. Young girls went up the hills and came home with armfuls of wildflowers. Nothing is too much trouble for an Anglican when he expects the Bishop.

The Bishop, accompanied by Mr. Cragg and a student, would

arrive for supper. It was the worst time of the year to prepare a special meal. Our last year's supplies were stale by now—eggs were overripe and butter had a rancid flavor. Fresh supplies were on the way, between Quebec and Mutton Bay, but that did not help the situation. However on the Coast there is always the freshest of fish. Crispy fresh capelin always tempted me, so I decided the Bishop might have the same taste.

Anxiously I watched the sun sink below the horizon and the misty haze which heralded twilight. One hour after we expected them, a strange motor was heard and the beehive colony frantically scurried about with last-minute preparations.

I had never witnessed a confirmation service; it was impressive and solemn. Eleven boys and girls, whom I knew intimately, were confirmed. The following morning, the Bishop and Mr. Cragg left for the next harbor and life settled back to its normal routine.

From intimate contact one learns to enter into the joys, suffering, anxieties, and sorrows of others. Here, as nowhere else, nature has to be contended with as well as enjoyed. We learn to meet each situation as it arises, treat each obstacle at a time, and as in Biblical days, say, "With God all things are possible." There is a constant test of faith which strengthens and upholds through all emergencies without leaving too great a scar on the heart.

Fathers, brothers, husbands, and sons sail out in the morning. Mothers, daughters, and sisters have faith that they will return with the setting sun. Although the ocean takes a terrible toll of lives, yet night after night sees most of these weary fishermen returning to their patiently waiting womenfolk. Their simple faith, their complete confidence in their religion, their loyalty to it, and the satisfaction they get from this loyalty upholds them even through the worst troubles and disasters.

One fine summer day, unable to locate a boat to answer an emergency call, I consulted Mr. Cragg and he volunteered to take me to the patient. As usual, other passengers also booked passage. Sitting or standing on deck, we enjoyed every moment of the lovely voyage over the calm rippling water to Whale Head.

It was not necessary for me to remain with the patient. I left medicine and instructions for home treatment. One mile out on our homeward journey we struck deep water and, as if from nowhere, like those sudden gales on the Sea of Galilee, a windstorm broke around us in great fury. The small boat was not built for rough water, and we pitched, lurched, and tossed alarmingly. One huge breaker lifted our boat on its crest and threw her forward onto the next breaking wave. Broadside, with a terrific smack, we struck the wave as another from behind broke with full force over the deck, washing everything before it and soaking us to the skin. As if rebelling at such rough treatment, the engine gave three kicks, sputtered, and died. Now we were really at the mercy of the sea. Another white-capped wave threatened to swamp the boat, but she managed to balance on the wave, roll sideways, then right herself before we were completely submerged.

From the engine room, Arthur, the boatman, shouted, "The trigger plug is gone."

Motorboats seldom leave home without towing a kinoo behind so that, in case of emergency, passengers may row ashore.

When we left, the day was ideal and we expected to be away only a short time, so we did not bring a tow-kinoo. Now we realized what a mistake it was to take such a chance.

In a tense voice Arthur shouted, "Wes'll never keep her right side up. Wes too far out at sea to make shore. Any minute may be our last."

With a clergyman and a missionary aboard offering prayers, would we get a direct or an indirect answer in time to save our lives?

Arthur called, "Has anyone a safety pin?" His strained voice was more urgent than frightened.

My mother taught me never to pin my clothes together. Hundreds of times she warned me, "A stitch in time saves nine." Fortunately for us, since I left home and practised nursing, with safety pins so handy, I had not followed her wise teaching.

I ducked into the cabin and was back in a jiffy with a strong safety pin. As another wave lashed the boat, the engine sputtered, the boat righted itself, and the engine gave a series of put-t-ts, then burrs followed by the regular hum of the motor. We had been saved by a safety pin. Never since have I left on a boat or dog-team trip without carrying a safety pin with me for luck.

This may have been an act of Providence, but Providence alone can do little unless one is prepared beforehand and ready to think and act quickly and efficiently. The boatman was a good-living, sincere Christian youth, quiet, quick, resourceful, and able to adapt himself to this emergency. Many men would have thrown up their hands in despair and exclaimed, "It is God's will." Arthur's calmness and fortitude had been developed during those long sitting-waiting-hours—waiting for wind, weather, and sea to let him launch his boat. Patiently and uncomplainingly he would sit and wait, knowing that all in good time the wind would drop, the weather would clear, and the sea would subside just as quickly as if he fretted. Yet when need arose, that reserve of knowledge developed during the long periods of waiting was put into action with marvellous speed. Perhaps those were not wasted hours and the subconscious mind was doing more valuable work than if he had been out with his boat.

The day after our stormy voyage was scorching hot. By noon the leaves on the shrubs hung limp and dry and the short-stemmed ferns drooped on the parched moss. Dogs sprawled on the rocks, panting with their tongues hanging out. Men worked with their shirt fronts open while drops of perspiration dripped from their foreheads and chins and oozed down their hairy chests.

All about us was cold, shark-infested water in which it was not safe to take a bath. The woolly odor from winter underwear still clung to my body and I pined for a dip in fresh water.

After dinner three small girls came to see if I could be persuaded to go up the hill to a fresh water pond in the rocks. Apparently this pool was there every spring, left by melting snow from above. Their mothers would not let them go alone but if the schoolteacher or I would go with them it was all right. Miss Wood and I did not need much coaxing.

At that time bathing suits were practically unknown to Coast children. The teacher and I had ours so we sent the girls home for makeshift suits. Alice came running back with a ragged, outgrown white flannellette nightgown which covered most of her body to her knees. Jane was swinging a pair of old pink silk bloomers, which covered her lower extremities. Mary dangled an old-fashioned house apron.

We climbed and clawed our way up the rocks, perspiration streaming from our necks and backs. The heat of the rocks almost blistered our feet despite our rubber-soled shoes. At the top of the first ridge of rocks, we had to cross a portage carpeted with soggy moss and we sank ankle-deep into the spongy bog. After crossing five hundred feet of this, we again crawled over the rocks. At every step water squashed between my parboiled, tender toes. After what seemed like miles, we reached the south side of the pond to find a perfect sandy beach and crystal-clear, blue water. A few feet across the pond the whole shore was covered with ice. We had earned a bath. Ice or no ice, we intended to have one. Each of us scurried to a private dressing room. Mine was behind a spruce shrub and the branches made satisfactory coat hangers. In a few minutes, garbed in our various suits, we stood and gazed into the icy water. Alice, the bravest, waded out three feet then ducked under, her nightgown ballooning about her. Jane waded in to her waist. Her tight, wet silk bloomers clung to her, giving her the appearance of a sleek seal. I expected to see flippers emerge on both sides. I dipped one big toe into the water, shivered, drew back, then simultaneously Miss Wood and I mustered courage to make a sudden dash. We took a deep breath, plunged under, and in a second came up sputtering water, shivering, and with chattering teeth. That was the coldest but most refreshing dip I ever took. Blue-lipped and with gooseflesh bodies, we sprawled on the rocks and let the hot sun stream over us until perspiration again oozed through our pores.

I had been sighing for the hot baths of the city, but none of them ever gave me the stimulating feeling I got from that bath under the open sky, cooled by ice and warmed by the sun.

The children also were pimpled with gooseflesh, but they ducked and played about in the water, apparently immune to the icy coldness. After ten minutes we felt they had been in long enough. Reluctantly, although shivering, they scrambled out onto the hot rocks. Then in a few minutes, their little bodies tingling with warmth, their tongues loosened, their eyes sparkling, they chattered like monkeys as they frisked along beside us.

When we left them each shyly asked, "Wes'll come again soon, won't wese?"

We arrived home to find the village in a whirl of excitement. Everywhere men talked excitedly in small groups. Women busily baked bread and beans. Boats were being overhauled and motors tested.

When God led the Israelites out of Egypt He did not forget that they needed physical nourishment. Sometimes the people on the Labrador Coast do not know where their next meal may come from and yet it always comes. Even today, miracles may happen. Word had come that a wrecked Norwegian steamer was sinking and would have to be abandoned. The law of the sea allows anyone to get what he can before the vessel sinks. Barrels of flour, butter, jam, lard, and apples were there for the taking. There was no time to be lost because boats were putting out from every harbor, each man hoping he might be the first to reach the wreck and the first to claim the choice salvage goods. Every man in Mutton Bay set out supplied with enough bread, beans, and lard for several days away from home. Two days later they returned, their boats laden with good things. This would be a backlog for the next winter's food.

A fisherman's life is either a feast or a famine. There is little halfway life for him. This was a feast, food dropped from heaven, free to all. You can imagine the welcome!

Time had flown so quickly I could not realize that it was a year since I had come to relieve Sister Martin. I was due to go out on the steamer which would dock in Mutton Bay the nearest to the fifteenth of August.

On the fifteenth, word came that we might expect the steamer on the sixteenth. That night we worked until midnight closing accounts and patients' records. Annie was going with me as far as Quebec City. We were taking with us her three-year-old nephew, Gordon, whose mother had died at another harbor. He had lived with us at the Station the last three weeks. I was to leave him with his uncle in Quebec, who later would take him to his grandparents in New Brunswick.

By ten o'clock the next morning we had our baggage at the kitchen door ready to take off at a moment's notice. Finally, at four o'clock, the telegraph operator got a message that the steamer was fogbound somewhere east of us. We ate some canned food and went to bed that night without removing our clothing.

Sunday morning the fog was so thick we could almost cut it, so we went to morning service. The service closed with everyone heartily singing, "God be with you till we meet again."

As I strolled home from church I wondered if we would meet

again. These people had become my people, part of my life, and my first choice would have been to stay with them. We slept in our clothes again that night, ready to leave instantly.

All day Monday, we could not get any report of the steamer's whereabouts. At midnight, fully clothed, hungry, expectant, and fatigued, we curled up on top of our beds. Tuesday morning at five o'clock Uncle John shouted upstairs, "Herns rounding the point. There be no time to lose." We grabbed our coats, took our baggage, and locked the Station door. Tugging Gordon between us, Annie and I, surrounded by youngsters and dogs, clambered over the rocks. At the wharf, nearly half the village had gathered to bid us farewell. Amid tears, shouts, handshakes, handkerchief waving, and last good-byes, we slid down the ladder to Uncle John's boat and soon drew alongside the steamer. We scrambled up the swinging ladder to the deck and stood waving until the steamer rounded the point and the village was lost from view.

It had been a tremendously strenuous, interesting, educational, and fascinating year. My philosophy of life had deepened and altered as I had rubbed shoulders with these simple people. From now on selfish motives would be sublimated. Never again could I wholeheartedly enjoy some of the superfluous luxuries previously considered necessities. Always there would flash through my mind the thought: Why should I spend so much for a coat when a cheaper one would be just as serviceable? Starving fishermen were struggling to eke out a living. Could it be Christian to parade vanity?

I left the Coast humbler, wiser, richer, and sincerely hoped that the benefit had not been all one-sided. Perhaps I had shared with them some of my knowledge and experience.

That night lying in a deck chair under the stars, I watched the beautiful northern lights twinkling and scintillating in the sky. Relaxed, without a care in the world, visiting with tourists from the outside world, we chugged over the salt water. For the first time in a year, free from night calls, I revelled in two dreamless nights.

The third night, we were wilted and groggy when we reached the dining room. Annie, Gordon, and I spent most of the next day huddled together, feeling exceedingly seasick and sorry for ourselves. At six o'clock that evening we docked at Clarke City. After a five minute promenade on land, and after long deep breaths of fresh air, the miseries of the day were forgotten.

At Clarke City, Gordon, who had been shy and had walked about or sat on my lap, suddenly exclaimed with wide-open, solemn, black eyes, "Look at the big doggie!" On the wharf stood a horse. In Gordon's life all animals, except rabbits and seals, had been dogs; he had never seen any other animals.

At Quebec City, Gordon's eyes nearly popped out of his head at the sight of streetcars, automobiles, buses, and bicycles rushing about the streets. I expected to hear him scream when our taxi started; he never uttered a sound but in order not to miss a thing looked alertly from one side to the other.

His grandmother, who had raised thirteen children, had left the Coast the previous fall and had seen, for the first time, the same things that her grandson now saw: streets, roads, cows, horses, cars, and trains.

When I delivered Annie and Gordon to her brother, all Coast responsibility dropped from my shoulders.

Feeling like Rip Van Winkle, and reeking with fish odors, I sought the Young Women's Christian Association and a bath.

After a luxurious tub, shampoo, haircut, wave, and movie, I took the train for home.

My relatives sniffed me as they would have sniffed a skunk, insisted that I smelled of codfish and made me hang my clothes outside for several days. I decided that no one who lived on the Coast could ever leave it behind. I apparently carried some of its characteristic odors in my clothes—they would soon disappear. But I was certain that I carried away in heart and mind something fine and indestructible.

part two: 1942

LABRADOR is mysterious beauty, pioneering adventure, deep-sea fishing, screaming gulls, mushing dog-teams, sailing boats, sputtering motors, trailing kinoos, greasy seal blubber, fish odors, and hospitable fisherfolk. And once again this Labrador beckoned to me. An emergency call had come for a nurse to take charge of the Mutton Bay district for a year. Once again I had to make ready to voyage down the great River and Gulf, this time on the *Sable Island*, which had replaced the *North Shore*.

During the intervening years I had worked with new Canadians and Indians in Western Canada. I had come to Toronto for further study. In May, 1942, I would be finished with my studies and I was contemplating a new adventure which would need several years to complete. On the twenty-sixth of May I came home to The United Church Training School. As I passed the wicket on the way to my room, I picked up my mail. The gong had rung so I tossed the letters on my bed and went down to dinner. After dinner I casually tore open the letters, little thinking that one of them was to change the whole course of my life. I read: "Our nurse has to leave Mutton Bay immediately and we are unable to find one to relieve her. Mutton Bay Station will be closed by the time this reaches you. Unless you come it will remain closed. You know the district. Can you take the next boat, which leaves in ten days?" The letter was from the secretary of the Grenfell Mission.

It was wartime and nurses were scarce everywhere. But these Coast people were so isolated and without dentists, doctors, nurses, or hospitals. This was a decision not to be made lightly. After two days of prayer and thought I wired Ottawa: "Will take the next steamer."

Although I knew what supplies I would need because of my previous years in Labrador, finding them was a problem. Toronto was sweltering in a heat wave and stores were not stocked with heavy woollen underwear, sweaters, socks, and rubber boots. In my spare time, I visited out-of-the-way stores, bargain sales, hounded perspiring clerks, tramped sun-baked sidewalks, wedged into crowded streetcars, and lugged home bulky boxes until I had a trunk full of woollens.

On the seventh of June I went to Montreal, expecting to sail the next morning. Our country was at war; submarines were in the Gulf and at the very mouth of the St. Lawrence River.

For the first time I realized that I would be travelling over guarded water and that every move must be made in deepest secrecy. I telephoned the steamship company's office and asked what time the *Sable Island* would leave the next day. Over the wire a voice answered, "Who are you?" I explained that I was the nurse booked to sail the next day. "Lady," said the voice, "we cannot give you any information over the wire, but you will not sail tomorrow or the next day. Come down to the office and see me." There I learned that the *Sable Island* had not returned from her last eastern trip and that no one knew what day she would dock. Also, that no reservations had been made. Furthermore every berth had been reserved for a group of government surveyors.

More and more I began to realize how inconvenient and hazardous war had made travelling. Everything and every person voyaging across water moved or stopped at a word from the Admiralty.

Still I hoped for a last minute cancellation. Early each morning I haunted the shipping office. On the night of the twelfth, tired, discouraged, and disgusted I went back to my hot room. My landlady handed me a telegram which read: "Do not leave on the *Sable Island*. Our boat, the *Nellie Cluett*, is calling at Montreal. Be ready to leave at any moment. Keep telephoning our office for last minute information. We cannot wire date of sailing because everything depends on the Admiralty."

Three days later, to my astonishment, the secretary replied, "She's in, come down and see the captain."

The captain was a man of few words. "We sail when the Admiralty says 'Go,' " he told me, "but bring your baggage down early tomorrow morning."

Overnight, a pea-soup fog enveloped the city and the misty

air penetrated to the bones. Fog or no fog, the *Nellie Cluett* was in harbor and I had to crawl out of my warm bed because the Admiralty might say "Go." Had I not waited long enough for this day?

My sister and brother-in-law called for me and soon we drew up at the wharf, but the globule-laden fog seemed determined that I should not mistake this for a pleasure cruise. We were walled in with the heavy, damp curtain. We could discern a dirty-grey steamer which resembled a shapeless ghost as it rocked and swayed and bumped against the wharf.

Captain Erick, a tall, angular, weather-worn Scandinavian with high cheek bones, a wavy shock of yellow-grey hair, and a ruddy complexion, gazed at us with frank eyes, which reminded me of the far-off blue sea. They managed to twinkle but his face wore a worried expression as he gave us permission to wander over the boat. The *Nellie Cluett* was not at all like the *North Shore*. She was owned and operated exclusively by and for the Grenfell Mission; she was built to carry freight but had several small cabins for Mission workers. Previously, Captain Erick had sailed her between Halifax, Newfoundland, and New York. Recently the Admiralty had ordered him to ply only in the waters of the Gulf and St. Lawrence River.

We soon completed our tour of inspection and I said farewell to my relatives. For another day painters and electricians worked at top speed to meet Admiralty requirements: the whole boat must be painted grey and re-wired so that when doors opened inward the lights would automatically be extinguished. But at long last the pilot came aboard and we heard the welcome order to weigh anchor.

The voyage down the great river was interesting but we were

never allowed to forget that our country was at war. The *Nellie* made few stops and, sooner than I had thought possible, I could see the landmarks that indicated our approach to Mutton Bay.

As we came closer to those familiar moss-clad, bleak rocks I was swept by a strong emotion. I had heard that the sea gets into one's blood. I felt that now. And I felt, too, a great liking, a genuine friendliness, for the people I had come once more to serve.

Hemmed in by apartment walls, stifled by stuffy germ-laden air, working with restless self-satisfied people who were always rushing about to provide security for themselves, I had somehow forgotten what to expect when I returned to Mutton Bay.

Now as I breathed the fresh, invigorating air, memories of my life in this little village were vivid and satisfying. It would be good to be once more with these fisherfolk—to enter into their joys and sorrows, be a part of their lives. I remembered Uncle John, a striking example of enterprise, perseverance, and co-operation, and all those others who patiently did their best whether it was skinning a seal, raising a fish net, driving a dog-team, or steering a boat. Free, independent, fine people they were. I was glad to be back.

We dropped anchor and I climbed down to a waiting boat. Once again Uncle John was there to welcome me; we headed shoreward while the *Nellie Cluett* swung out to sea. Shouts of, "See you on the Coast this winter!" "Stop in if down our way," "Bon voyage!" and "God speed you!" were interchanged with fellow-passengers and members of the crew until the *Nellie* passed out the channel and was lost to view round the rocks.

Annie was no longer at the Station. A new maid, Mary, and Sam, a chore boy, and I were soon busy completing the cleaning.

It was just as well we did so, for early next morning a gun blew the end off a finger which had pulled a trigger out of season. Before I finished dressing the wound Mr. George rushed over to the station shouting, "Sister, come quickly the baby is about here."

After that first day, I was again part of the village, almost an old-timer. I spent the entire second day visiting in the village homes getting "caught up" with all that had happened during my years of absence. Accounts of births, deaths, and marriages came first; it was sad to learn that some old friends were missing —but that was to be expected—and there were new babies to admire and stories to hear of the boys and girls who had grown up since my departure.

A great many interesting things had happened in the intervening years. In the evenings I pieced the stories together and the picture they gave me of present-day Labrador was a heartening one.

It was essentially the same Mutton Bay village as in 1928, yet different in many ways. I realized already—and more fully in the days that followed—that much progress had been made since I had last been here. The people had been in a starving condition so the government had come to the rescue. It did not issue direct relief but required each man to do some work in return for help. Where previously there had been nothing but mud, we now had sand walks and several gravel paths with corduroy bridges over low muddy and swampy ground. Formerly, dogs and children had run over the rocks where fish were drying; now many of the fishermen had built fishing flakes.

In 1928 there were practically no gardens; now some of the villagers had a few flowers, radishes, lettuce, and turnip greens, and others had carried down enough earth from the hills to grow carrots and potatoes. The seeds had been issued to them by the government. As a result, there were fewer undernourished children, fewer rickety legs and tummies and perhaps less tuberculosis and skin diseases, while beriberi had been wiped out.

The overseas demand for fish had caused the price of all types of fish to soar. This made it possible for the people to purchase a greater variety of food for their own use. Butter, vegetables, sugar, and meat had been added to their diet of fish, berries, molasses, flour, oatmeal and lard. In 1928 no milk had been available; now cocoa and canned milk were purchased for some of the children.

Government positions—surveyors, local men for rough jobs or to work as gamewardens, bird inspectors, fish inspectors, and extra mail carriers—had mushroomed in a few months. This meant a deeper interest in better educational standards and a slightly higher scale of living. Also, it meant more nourishing food, warmer and prettier clothing for all the family. Where once they had merely existed, some of the women actually began to enjoy life.

Many of the boys from this part of Labrador had been called to military service. Letters from these boys linked the isolated Coast people with the rest of the world. This resulted in a greater knowledge of other parts of Canada and the rest of the Commonwealth, even of far-off Japan and China.

But the Coast, I believe, will always retain its own identity, for the people are strongly loyal to the traditions handed down from generation to generation.

TOWARD the end of my first week at the Station I was aroused at four o'clock in the morning by a man's voice shouting, "Sister, get up. Baby case."

When I came downstairs, warmly dressed I thought, for what might be ahead of me, Mr. Mason informed me it would be a six-mile boat trip so I added two more sweaters and took my rubber coat and sou'wester. Even in June, snowbanks and icebergs make the weather uncertain and the air very cold. When we pushed off from the wharf hardly a ripple stirred the surface of that crystal-clear salt water. I leaned over the edge of the boat and far below saw tiny fish swimming about among the starfish and clams which were imbedded in the mud.

The shore rose into a perpendicular cliff hundreds of feet above the water's edge. High up on the peaks of the rugged cliffs, gulls balanced on one leg as they dozed waiting for the herring to run, when they would come to life and dive for their breakfasts. At the bottom of the sea, early small fish scurried hither and yon in a frantic effort to secure their breakfast before larger fish, gulls, and crows wakened.

I gazed out on the miles of clear, blue watery expanse which ended in a mirage of wakening horizon, then deep below into the depth of the sea overshadowed by the tall cliffs, and awe and reverence for some mighty, majestic Power so great I could not begin to conceive of its grandeur filled my mind. How minute seemed man and man's power!

My daydreaming was ended abruptly by that well-remembered thump as we bumped the rubber-tire shock absorber on the side of the wobbly, half-fallen-away wharf.

The previous night a baby girl had been born to a mother already so worn-out with child-bearing and undernourishment that she did not have the necessary strength to complete the job. It was my duty to finish the process by delivering a retained placenta. Always before in my experience this had been the work of a doctor.

I collected my sterile equipment and attempted to recall what doctors had done in similar circumstances. Mrs. George was frantically counting her rosary, while her sister, weeping and wringing her hands in agony, knew the patient was going to die. Confidently (inwardly less confident) I assured this Job's comforter that Mrs. George would soon be all right. Sometimes

God works in a mysterious way; suddenly came the inspiration what to do next. I set to work and half an hour later the patient was laughing and chatting with the family. Her husband went off to spread the good news through the village and she tucked her rosary under her pillow.

Homeward bound, I resumed my interrupted musings. We passed narrow ravines with moss-covered tops in which flowers desperately clung. Tiny fishing shacks nestled on and among the rocks. Trickling streams dripped from shrub-covered ledges down hundreds of feet of sheer cliffs to the yawning chasms between rugged rocks at the bottom.

As we passed a westbound boat, a loud "Hullo!" came across the water. Half a mile farther on a man shouted, "Good catch today?" As we drew near the Station a fisherman shouted, "How's the patient? Will hern make it? What did hern get this time?"

The sun dipped to bed in the western horizon leaving a beautiful afterglow. How I longed to be an artist so that I might capture in permanent form the lovely colors! Our boat spanked the waves as they rebounded from the shore, then we drifted lazily to the wharf. As I climbed the rocks to the Station I could hear the putt-putt of motorboats wending their way shoreward and see dimly a sailboat or two slowly drifting toward home as noiselessly as the gulls. Across the water, came the call of a loon and screams of dozens of gulls. The night breeze died away, and, just as I reached the Station, darkness settled over the whole hillside.

The peace and beauty of the evening was reflected within me. I was filled with high aspiration and hope.

In the first weeks I heard a great deal about a new visitor to Mutton Bay who had come the last two summers and for whose return many of the younger women and girls were looking forward eagerly—the beauty specialist. She was expected some time in August. I could not feel enthusiastic about her work: much of the hair she had treated was straggly and lifeless-looking, no longer natural and beautiful.

A permanent on the Coast, without electricity or running water, is really an event. The lady with her machineless apparatus went, I was told, from place to place by fishing boats. When she arrived at the first village she enquired about until she found a fisherman who was going to the next village, then she interviewed his wife and offered to give her a free wave in return for a safe voyage to the next harbor. Usually she made a quick deal. Next she located a prominent place in the adjoining village to set up her apparatus. When she found a suitable place she sent word to the woman that she would give her a free wave for the use of her home. Occasionally she had to throw in a free wave for the daughter as well.

All this accomplished, she contacted the two prominent broadcasters, the postmistress, and the telegraph operator. They always knew approximately when she would reach their village. Frequently it is late at night when fishing boats return home. Even so, customers would be waiting and she would work far into the night, stopping at intervals to book customers for the next day.

Still, a permanent is an exciting event. There is no running water, electric drier, or drainage, just vanity and nature. One by one, the beauty operator shampoos women and sends them home to dry their hair. If it is a rainy day the victims have to huddle on the floor in front of their kitchen stoves until the hair is thoroughly dry, then borrow a sou'wester or waterproof for their heads and row back for the final transformation. If it is a sunny day, nature does the drying in a short time.

As street urchins in the city watch every chance to earn a few cents, so here small boys watch their opportunities and one or two of them are ready, with their kinoos, to row customers across the tickle.

Men, women, and children flock to this amateur beauty parlor and stand or sit about. At first, too loyal to tradition to show any interest openly, the older fishermen seek some excuse to stroll in and stare at the customer being transformed while they mutter comments under their breath about this young generation and its frivolities. The middle-aged women stare with longing eyes, and the young folk giggle and nudge each other while they wait their turn.

When her work is finished the lady leaves for the next village. In a few months there may be some woebegone heads, some complaining customers, but by the time the hair magician comes again she will stir up the same excitement and dozens will flock to her door.

At Mutton Bay it is never a question of which doctor or nurse is the best. There is only one nurse available and her patients consult her not from choice but from necessity. In 1942 I never needed to wonder if patients would come, because they came at all hours.

During the next few months there were hours of suspense

when, dissatisfied with my own diagnosis and not pleased with the progress of my patient, yet doing my best under the circumstances, I wondered what the result would be.

Frequently it was extremely hard to make a correct diagnosis without seeing the patient. I recall one rather indefinite diagnosis. A Mr. Whiter came in one afternoon and said, "Mrs. Segan asked me to call and get hern some medicine."

"What is her trouble?" I enquired. She was a newcomer in the district.

"Oh," he replied, "hern has a backache and herns legs pain hern and herns arms are weak and hern cannot eat."

"How old is she?" I questioned.

"Let me see, I guess herns must be about sixty-two, more or less."

"How long has her back bothered her?"

"Oh, for years."

"How many years?"

"Oh, probably twenty or thirty or longer, or probably not as long as herns legs, or it could be longer."

"Has she more pain than she had twenty years ago?"

"Oh, yes, herns gets worse each year."

"Has she ever seen a doctor?"

"Oh, yes, herns always sees him when hes goes through."

"Does he give her any medicine?"

"Oh, yes, hes very kind and always gives hern some medicine and pills to take and some liniment to rub on."

After a few more questions the diagnosis was made and Mr. Whiter carried home some cure-all drugs for her. He was satisfied that I knew her trouble and pleased to be able to help relieve her suffering. I heard later that her pains were much better and that she was happy about the new medicine. I realized once again that faith works miracles.

Another complicated history was that of a sick child. After trying to get Elsie's history from her mother I had to stretch my imagination to meet a baffling situation.

Emphatically Mrs. Leroux stated, "Oh no, hern is never sick, except at spells. Hern was always weak and not like my other children—yet hern was always well. Hern always had chills down herns back, especially on bitter cold days when the bedclothes slipped off and hern had on thin pyjamas, because hern will not wear warm pyjamas. But hern usually is hot when it is hot and when hern has lots of bedclothes. Hern eats when hern has an appetite."

I gave up attempting to diagnose the case from the past history, but made one more attempt to find the condition of her posture, which might indicate chest or spine trouble.

"Has she a good standing and sitting posture?"

"Oh, yes, hern has a fine position, but hern stoops badly at times, and one doctor told me herns had a crooked spine, and herns neck was twisted a little, but hern has always had a perfect posture. It can't be that."

I gave up and resorted to a theoretical diagnosis.

A third type of puzzling information for diagnostic purposes came over the telegraph wires. Prescribing, sometimes, was like taking a leap in the dark.

Mrs. Tucker, a neighbor, had seen Mrs. Legrand and thought she should see a nurse, so she went to her village operator, who could not speak or write English fluently. The operator got the diagnosis from Mrs. Tucker, then attempted to send it to me in code through our English operator. After a series of code messages, I grasped some idea of Mrs. Legrand's troubles. Again, through English-French code, I had to send orders for simple treatments which would not do any harm and, if carried out with any intelligence, might do some good. Later, I discovered that sometimes if I ordered heat to the feet or cold to the head, these might be reversed. One grandmother informed me, "We changed. The ice made hern head feel so good we knew it would help hern feet."

It did not take long to learn that diagnosing by means of telegram, letter, or a neighbor's account was very difficult, and prescriptions must be simple and harmless.

To criticize without knowing the facts seems to be a failing of human nature. At times my treatments were viciously attacked. Very few patients would do this to my face because I was the only nurse, kept the only drugs available, and they might have to seek me in emergency. Usually, if the patient was not satisfied with the treatment, he accepted it willingly, went home, ripped off the dressing, and treated it himself, or discontinued the medicine and set the bottle away in a dark corner in case he needed it for some other trouble later. Sooner or later, by that mysterious Coast grapevine, the story came back to me and was useful when more treatment was needed.

Soon I learned that the best policy was to ignore non-cooperation and not to let the patient know I had heard anything, but to give something that would not be much waste if thrown away. But I always told the truth tactfully and considerately to the relatives as far as they could comprehend it. In this way I got along very nicely with the majority of my patients.

On a sweltering Dominion Day, a Canadian holiday celebrated July 1, a boy came to the Station and said he had a "rizin finger." I had forgotten this word. One glance at the finger and I recalled these "galled fingers." His finger, resembling a frizzling sausage about to burst its jacket, was one of those overripe infected fingers which require immediate operation. Without any anæsthetic, grim and silent, he sat while I prepared a sterile field. Although I dreaded such an operation more than he did, I managed to conceal my feeling. I located the ripest spot, took a long breath, uttered a prayer for him and one for me, made a deep gash and held my breath. He wilted on to my shoulder. Pus spouted, like a geyser, in all directions. He was too heavy to lift so I braced my feet and supported him until he came to. He smiled, looked at his finger, and said, "O.K., Sister, hern doesn't hurt no more." I dressed the incision, he put on his cap, and went home. For both of us it was all in a day's work.

The next week brought another ripe finger but never again did I attempt such an operation with a sitting patient. He came in late in the afternoon and the infection was deep-seated. The finger looked like a squashy banana, three times its normal size. This was a case for a doctor and an anæsthetic, so I wired to the doctor, who replied, "Do the best you can under the circumstances."

With hope in my heart that it might burst or, at least come to a definite point, I swathed the whole hand in a huge, hot application. Mary, my maid, was out and would not return before ten o'clock that night. It was impossible to tackle such an operation alone and by lamplight. When she came in, Mr. Samuel was writhing and moaning in agony and the external spot was much softer. Mary was made of good stuff and agreed to hold the flashlight and, if necessary, continue with the local anæsthetic so that I would have both hands free for scalpel, swabs, and patient.

I started the anæsthetic, then instructed Mary how to carry on. A fisherman's finger is always calloused and tough. This infection was so deep-seated I had to go through the thick outer layer and down into the fleshy part. I remembered a doctor's instructions when assisting him with a similar case: "Make a wide gash and go deep." I went deep, straight, and wide. When I struck the pocket, the pus spouted and the pain ceased immediately. With trembling knees and white face, Mary rushed from the room. I offered a prayer of thankfulness, but the patient, exhausted after days of suffering, just turned over and went to sleep.

At dusk the second week in July, a boat from thirty miles down the Coast drew up to our wharf. A young man, Bill Clarke by name, came over to the Station. "Ise hasn't slept for three days and nights with toothache. Will yous pull hern for me so that Ise can go back fishing tonight?"

Having had previous experience with those long-rooted, black-cavitied, shell-edged teeth, I remembered the crunch of the outer decayed rims when the forceps were applied. I had seen the dentist take out such a tooth, piece by piece, under local anæsthetic and did not want to tackle this one alone; but what could I do? It would be inhuman to send him back until a doctor might pass his way some months later. Something had to be attempted. As frequently happened, Uncle John appeared over the rocks. I explained to him that I was willing to apply the forceps but that I needed his wrist to do the hauling. "O.K.," he said, hung his cap on the back of Bill's chair, adjusted the wad of tobacco to his upper lip, and was ready for action.

Bill planted his feet firmly on the floor in front of him, gripped the chair with both hands, shut his eyes, threw back his head, and gasped, "Ready, Go!"

Before he knew what had happened, the tooth, roots and all, went flying through the air and struck the floor behind him.

Bill got to his feet, spat several times, thanked Uncle John and me, went back to his boat and set out for home. Although it was eight o'clock at night and he had not slept for three nights, he started eastward, thirty miles, to be ready at dawn for the first catch of fish. What was a tooth when his family depended on the fishing catch for their living?

The care of the sick, in these sparsely populated areas, still offers immeasurable difficulties. Rain and snowstorms rage with undiminished force. The treacherous, cracking spring and fall ice make travelling difficult or impossible. Many times, in order to get the doctor or nurse, the patient has to travel through blinding snow or beating rain, over pathless marshes, portages, over rocks or ice, and through deep snow, slob water, or mud. In most cases excruciating pain has been endured for days, weeks, or months, before the patient gets relief after risking the journey to the Station.

On the last Sunday morning in the month rain beat down in torrents. Mary was our organist, so we donned rubber boots, sou'westers, and raincoats over our Sunday clothes and waded to the church. We arrived as the first bell ceased ringing and left our streaming coats in the entry and went inside, she to the organ, and I to be the congregation.

From the ceiling came the constant drip of water, which plashed in trickling streams into various pews and coursed along the floor. Around the stovepipes rain streaked down in black rivulets. We sat for fifteen minutes but not another person entered the church. I was about to investigate whether service had been cancelled but my inspiration came too late. The clergyman, robed in his clerical gown, marched down the long aisle to the vestry. He went inside and announced, "We will sing Hymn Number 286, 'O Brothers, Lift Your Voices'." He closed the door and, as was the custom, gave one long pull on the bell cord. It pealed forth, telling all worshippers (me) that the service was about to commence. With the prayer book open in his hand, head bowed, he swished through the door and took his place beside the pulpit. The organ burst into "O Brothers, Lift Your Voices." It did not seem quite appropriate, since we two females were the entire congregation, but as we sang I remembered how Christ had foreordained comfort for people like us when He told His disciples, "Where two or three are gathered together in my name, there am I in the midst of them."

Mr. Meek went through the whole morning service, with me making all the responses, and then straight from the shoulder, with both eyes focused on me, he delivered a most personal and inspiring address.

Never before or since have I been the sole congregation with a half hour sermon delivered directly to my soul. It was a peculiar feeling not soon to be forgotten.

There was no coughing, fidgeting, or wriggling to disturb his or my concentrated attention. I am certain he would have been glad to have heard a baby cry, a sneeze, or a giggle. I would gladly have welcomed anything that might divert those eyes from me.

The next Sunday I suffered some embarrassment and disappointment.

Thursday night a message came from the doctor saying, "Head officials will be coming soon."

A visit, no matter how short, from an Off-coaster is a rare and appreciated treat. All day Friday we cleaned and scrubbed until Saturday night, satisfied that not a speck of dust would be spied, we went to bed. Sunday unofficial rumors kept coming in that the Mission boat was at Harrington Harbour, then that she had left there. When she did not come and we could not get any reports we gave up expecting her that night and I went to evening service. Before the clergyman entered the church Uncle John tapped my shoulder and whispered, "Shes left for here an hour ago."

Quietly I slipped out and rushed over to the Station. On extra special occasions we hoisted our flag, so for several days we had been practising flag raising. I got it half up the pole and there it stuck. It was barely halfway up but I decided that no one would think it was flying at half staff, so I pulled the cord and it unfurled with the breeze. After two hours I knew something was wrong because the boat should have arrived in Mutton Bay long before that.

At the telegraph office the operator informed me that the captain had decided not to call at Mutton Bay but had passed an hour ago, heading straight for Newfoundland. Disappointed at being deprived of the visit and rather embarrassed, I hauled down our flag. Also, I regretted having missed our service. I resolved never again to be too hasty flying a flag.

To compensate for missing our visitors with news from the outside world, I took a book and sat out on the steps to watch the sunset over the hills and tickle.

Human beings might disappoint us, boats might come and leave, but the sky never failed to provide us with ever-changing, awe-inspiring panorama of picturesque, colorful scenes. Blood-red, the sun sank behind the cove, its rays extending far across the tickle, then it blanketed itself behind the hills and trees and left behind a gently shifting, vast purple and gold afterglow. The stars appeared one by one until suddenly the whole sky was ablaze with silver lights, the crescent moon crept up from the horizon to add her share of beauty, and the northern lights danced and crackled and shone with their own special magnificence.

Then just as I was deciding to go inside there came the long expected and most welcome putt-putt of the local mail boat. Mail, parcels, and newspapers drove the last of my disappointment from my mind.

Tomorrow would be a new day!

FOR several days life had been monotonous and I longed for some excitement. Then the doctor arrived and commotion reigned. His box of medicines, dental instruments, eye-testing apparatus, and his sympathetic nature brought out all the chronic sufferers. Men, women, babies, grandparents, and young fishermen sat on the doorstep waiting to have their troubles diagnosed, cured, or treated. Teeth flew in all directions. Eyes were examined and fitted for new glasses. Ears were pulled forward, overhauled, and wax plugs syringed out. All cases had to be considered before the doctor could proceed on his journey and repeat the work in the next village. By the following afternoon the human machinery of the village seemed to be in working order again.

When Dr. Gray was ready for his boatman, a general shout was raised for Uncle Ed; then two boys set off in search of him. Soon they reappeared with Uncle Ed stumping along behind them. The doctor was taking with him an expectant mother from another harbor who was going to her mother's home to be confined. We waved them out of sight around the point.

At seven o'clock that night, as I sat in the kitchen bathing Teddy, our little patient, I heard a great commotion on the rocks above the Station. Then someone shouted, "Sister, Sister, quick, the doctor is in trouble. His boat is going round in circles and he is hoisting and lowering his flag signalling for help." Mrs. Bray was frantically waving her arms and shouting for me.

Shortly after the doctor left we had heard what sounded like a plane in distress. Now I pictured the doctor returning with one or two battered men whom he had picked up from the wreckage. I handed Teddy to Mary and instructed her to get him to bed as quickly as possible, to put on plenty of hot water, and to stand by in case of emergency. Teddy, suspecting he would miss something, opened his mouth and let out one of his unforgettable howls, which added to the commotion.

I hastened over the rocks, fastening up my boat togs as I went. An excited woman stopped me and said, "I knows Mary has had her baby on the boat and the doctor wants yous." It was Mary's first baby so I knew differently.

Men and women were gathered in small groups, all talking at the same time. I shouted to two of the men to follow along in case they would be needed to carry a stretcher. When we reached the wharf, there was Dr. Gray sitting on the edge of the Mission boat talking with Uncle Ed and Mary, the expectant mother. When he saw me he shouted, "What's all the excitement? Has there been an accident?"

"You are the accident," I replied. "They came rushing for me shouting that you were in trouble, going round in circles, so I presumed you must have gone insane and needed help."

I can still see Dr. Gray's face when he heard that. He sat there on the edge of the boat and nearly split his sides laughing. Mary threw back her head and burst into laughter too.

When the doctor could control his voice he explained. "We left the open harbor and found the sea too rough to proceed, so we put into the cove and had supper. Coming back, we decided to unfurl our boat flag, and somehow the rope got tangled about the pole, so we let the boat drift, apparently in circles, while we worked with it. We have come back to sleep at the Station and will go on tomorrow."

Every time later on when I visited her harbor, Mary recalled the excitement she had given Mutton Bay people—more indeed than she gave Harrington people when her daughter actually made her debut into this world.

August was an exceptionally busy month, for in addition to the routine nursing and confinements this was the time of preparation for Christmas. I found it a delightful yet complicated and tiring task. Things worked this way: each year the Mutton Bay nurse must prepare and send a toy, a bag of candy, and a card to about six hundred children in twelve isolated villages along the Coast. The Mission supplies the articles, but the nurse has to sort the toys, choose appropriate gifts, and allot exactly the same amount of candy for each child. The local mailman takes the parcels, free of charge, provided the parcels are wrapped in separate bundles, well labelled, and ready before the first of September. After this date travel is uncertain and treacherous. Whenever he has extra space in his boat he picks up a bundle and leaves it with the schoolteacher or some reliable person, who distributes the articles at Christmas time.

Decisions were often difficult. It would never do to send a six-year-old fisherman's son a doll's cradle, or a Roman Catholic girl, who could not read English, a Presbyterian hymnal. But was I to know the sex or denomination of Bettex, Donnit, Leslie, Francis, Ewist, or Twilly? I recall one instance when a young nurse gave an absolutely penniless, completely bald, elderly lady a pretty red purse and a red comb to match. She was delighted with them, and although the purse was empty and the comb not usable, each night she took them to bed with her.

After an open fall, Labrador winter set in with a vengeance. For two weeks, men had ganged up as man power to haul their boats ashore. It requires eight, ten, or twelve men, according to the size of the boat and the distance of the haul from the water to a safe spot on the shore. All boats have to be hauled out in the fall and to the water's edge in spring over sandy or rocky shore. They have to be safe when the ice starts to form and when the tide washes seaward or huge ice cakes would smash them to tinder and the tide would carry them out to sea.

The seventh of November, after a busy day, a quiet evening seemed possible, so I lighted the fire in the fireplace and settled down to get my mail ready for our last mail boat of the fall. Before I had finished one letter the telegraph operator came with a message from the doctor. "Can you go on an emergency case? I cannot leave."

The call had come from the east more than a hundred miles down the Coast. The doctor was tied up with a maternity case, I learned later, so had wired for me to answer this call. Winter was upon us; nearly all the boats had been hauled up. The round trip would mean approximately two hundred and twenty-five miles, with several nights aboard a boat. At this time of year distance is difficult to compute. One has to reckon with the sea and the weather. We might make ten or we might make fifty miles in one day, or there was a possibility that we might not make fifteen miles and have to turn back or be stranded several days anywhere along the Coast.

No cabin boats were available in Mutton Bay. I wired to two other villages but was unsuccessful. No man would dare risk the trip in an open boat, because if we should get caught in a storm, we should certainly freeze to death. After trying for two hours with no luck, I had to wire the doctor, "No cabin boat available."

At eleven o'clock that night he wired back, "Cabin boat located. Boatman willing to attempt trip at daylight tomorrow. Will call for you." This meant a night's delay in starting to answer an emergency call.

The next morning, swathed in woollen undervests, sweaters, leather jacket, waterproof dickie, woollen socks, and rubber boots, I waited for the boat. By eleven o'clock, I resembled a parboiled wild goose and was beginning to grow anxious about the boatman.

At noon another wire came from the doctor. "Terrific sea in Harrington makes travel impossible today." Our water, only thirty miles away, was calm and peaceful. When he learned that we were not in the grip of the storm he wired to me again.

This emergency case should have had medical treatment the previous Tuesday. It was Friday, the patient was suffering agonies, and even if we wired instructions there was no available equipment to relieve him.

On Saturday morning I got into the same paraphernalia and waited. At one o'clock the boat docked and I went aboard. It was Mr. James, the bird inspector, with his son and boat. Many times, over almost impassable seas, he had risked his life to save someone else's life. That day the wind was with us and the boat sailed along like a graceful swan. We made six miles an hour until darkness set in at five o'clock. About four o'clock Mr. James said to his son, "Soon we must find a sheltered cove where we can anchor for the night."

Sunburned, grimy, fascinated, steaming in woollens, and at the same time shivering with cold, I enjoyed the trip. Sometimes I stood beside the boatman on the open deck and at other times I huddled close to the cabin stove. Once, for fifteen minutes, Mr. James let me take the wheel.

As twilight approached Mr. James and Tom discussed the merits of each cove. Would a sudden northern blizzard sweep through that cove? Were there any dangerous shoals hiding beneath the water in this cove? Would the anchors hold here? What about this one? Always the same questions until I began to wonder if any cove would have all the required points. Then we ran into one which met Mr. James' approval and he shouted to Tom, "Drop anchor."

We had one cabin, approximately six by ten feet, in which there was a stove, table, two berths, a swinging lamp, two men and me, plus our extra clothing, wood, food, and supplies, but with absolutely no privacy. Mr. James knew that this was my first long-distance, close-quarters, non-private minus-necessities trip, so casually he remarked, "Tom and I will go out on deck while you get ready for bed."

Quickly I stripped off a few outer layers, crawled under and among blankets, snuggled down, turned my face to the wall, and shouted, "All right." The two men climbed into the other narrow bunk and loud snores soon told me that weariness had been forgotten. In a very short time I was sound asleep. My last thoughts were of woollen odors and a feeling of being cooked alive, because my feet nearly rested on the stove which Mr. James had crammed with wood before he crawled into bed.

At four o'clock in the morning I awakened shaking with cold and felt the dampness penetrating through every bone. My blankets had slipped to the floor. As quietly as possible I tugged at them; from under a mound of deerskin, Mr. James' muffled voice asked, "Are you cold? I will get up and light a fire." With chattering teeth I replied, "No, I'm all right, only the blankets and I parted company." Quickly he jumped across, tucked me in, and crawled back into his berth. Again all was quiet and the gr-whish of sonorous breathing told me that he was asleep. Like a cradle on the deep we swayed with the sea's rhythmic motion. Once more warmth crept into my body and I slept.

At five-thirty the men crawled out and Mr. James said, "You do not need to get up yet." Their breakfast, a large mug of boiled tea and a huge hunk of bread and butter, did not take long. The teapot was shoved to the back of the stove to be reheated again and again during the day. At seven o'clock Mr. James stuck his head through the door and shouted, "Better crawl out and have a mouthful before we get into loppy water." He knew my weakness as a sailor and how much better a seasick person's stomach operates if there is something in it when that awful feeling strikes.

I dashed some cold salt water on my face and was wide awake. The cabin reeked with multifarious boat odors, so I took my biscuits and a dish of dry cereal and made a quick exit to the fresh air on the open deck. It was one of those fine mornings with the invigorating tang of sea blowing across the water. There was a nip in the air as we cut our way through the waves that made it a joy to be alive. We dove deep into the watery trough, heaved forward, then rose onto the crest of the next whitecap, spanked down onto the green foam, then struck loppy water. The boat rolled to its side, was tossed high in the air, then righted itself and lurched forward. The water was icy green and the air was icy cold. In fact, everything from sea to sky, including myself, was green and icy. With a final lurch we planked onto calm water.

Mr. James was not familiar with the dangerous shore and reefs beyond Old Fort, so we stopped to pick up a pilot. By the time Tom had thrown the anchor overboard, Mr. James was over the edge and pushing off in a kinoo toward the shore. In a few moments he returned with a pilot. As I have said before, along the Coast everything and everybody is interested in everybody else. This man heard our need, closed his local store, and came to help us. He might be gone for a day, two days, or a week, but he would not take a cent for his services.

When the men cast anchor in the harbor of our destination, a blinding blizzard struck and snow fell all night. Had we been one hour later, we would have had to anchor outside indefinitely.

It was now Sunday afternoon. I took one look at Mr. Gadly, the patient, whose agonizing groans could be heard all over the home, and immediately knew that, without a couple of day's treatment, he would never live to reach a doctor or hospital. For several days he had been delirious from pain so I gave him a strong sedative and started a series of wires to the doctor, a hundred miles away. Over the wires we diagnosed and the doctor prescribed. When the patient was fairly well under the sedative, I started treatment and by seven o'clock that night he was rational and comfortable. By paracentesis, I released ninety ounces of fluid. Lest he collapse if I continued, I stopped treatment temporarily and let Mr. Gadly sleep for several hours before releasing more.

The temperature was dropping and the ice was catching in the tickle, so Mr. James and Tom slept aboard their boat in order to move it frequently to prevent its being wedged into an ice block.

Monday evening the weather turned much colder and Mr. James came ashore to inform me, "If yous wish to get out this fall we will have to leave at daybreak. If not, my boat will freeze solid and we will not be able to move until next spring."

Often it is hard to get telegraphic connections—particularly when they are urgently needed. I tried for several hours to reach the doctor for advice, then gave up and decided this was a time when I would have to depend on my own judgment. I explained the situation to Mrs. Gadly and left her to make the final decision. My heart ached for these people, but I could not give them much comfort or hope. The husband-father could not live long at home. He might die at any moment along the journey or he might not survive an operation. Coast mothers and wives have to face many stern realities with fortitude and calmness. I could not remain away from my Station and Mrs. Gadly could not leave her children, telegraph office, and post office to accompany her husband. He would have to set off on this uncertain trip with me, a stranger, in attendance.

I had a long talk with the family and explained that we could not guarantee anything. Also, that for the greater part of the trip we would not have any contact with the land for hours, perhaps days, and that we would have to travel with the weather and the sea. They knew what all this involved. I could assure them that God was with us on land and sea and that His great love would care for us wherever we were if we trusted ourselves in His merciful hands. After prayers and consultations, Mr. Gadly and his family felt that we should make an attempt to get him through to the hospital. We assured them that, God willing, we would get him there.

Late that night the men made a stretcher that would go through the cabin door and was large and strong enough to balance across a small kinoo on the way to the waiting motor-boat.

Early Tuesday morning, I gave Mr. Gadly a strong sedative and sent another wire to the doctor, informing him that we were starting for the hospital but we were unable to wait for a reply. I promised Mrs. Gadly that whenever there was an office where we stopped I would send her a message so that she would know how her husband was standing the trip.

We carried Mr. Gadly downstairs and placed him on the handmade stretcher, which the men carried to the water's edge and balanced across the kinoo. As we cut our way through shimmering ice to the boat Mr. James remarked, "What a perfect day! We should be able to reach some harbor where we can lift the stretcher ashore into a friendly home."

At four o'clock that afternoon Mr. James again remarked, "What an ideal day!" To which Mr. Gadly replied, "God has been with us to give us this day." At four-thirty, like a thunderbolt from a blue sky, a blizzard swooped down on us. The force of the gale swung the boat about and a wild sea faced us. In a few moments the boat was coated with ice and snow.

Mr. James shouted to Tom in a tense voice, "Nothing to do but find some sort of shelter and that quickly. The anchors will not hold here." Hastily Tom lashed everything to the deck. Like a hammock, the cabin lamp swung from side to side. The boat pitched forward, lurched backward, and then rolled broadside, all in one moment.

Outside was inky blackness that one feels rather than sees. A feeling of pending danger filled my soul. The sound of the waves grew louder and closer. I felt a dark blanket drawing itself around and over us. As we swayed, rocked, and plunged in the semishelter, we could hear the weird, unearthly roar of the sea and wind, followed by the loud boom of the breakers as they broke in fury against the rocks. Through that eerie darkness those booms sounded like angry cannons answering each other out of the depth of nowhere. As one died away in the distance, the next boom roared at its heels.

It was a ghastly business. Here we were, and here we stayed until two o'clock the next afternoon—an emergency patient facing death, every moment counting, not a relative aboard, no means of communication with land, and frequent treatments requiring a sterile needle and syringe. A swaying wood stove and a sliding basin in which to boil my sterile equipment did not help matters.

Wiry, wizened, tough, and more than sixty years of age, Mr. Gadly gazed patiently and courageously about the cabin. He had known all the hardships encountered in a life spent on the sea and he accepted his fate without complaints. His was an inner calm as he lay there awaiting his fate. His serene patience inspired me with a confidence and a strength which spurred me to do my best.

Outside, the foredeck was icy, wet, and slippery with briny spray swishing from every side, while overhead it was wild, black, and stormy. At ten o'clock the lines began to strain, so the men put on their waterproofs and went out to tighten them. When they returned their rubber clothing left trails of icy salt water on our cabin floor. Their red faces dripped with salt water. A constant drip, drip, came from the cabin roof as water slowly soaked our blankets and mattresses.

Bedtime came. The men spread a deerskin and blankets on the floor of the cabin for me. In this way, I was within reach of Mr. Gadly without having to disturb the other two men. If they had slept on the floor and I had taken the berth, I should have had to climb over them every time I had to treat the patient. There was little room for extra feet to move about on the floor, but it was dry and free from drafts.

Mr. James was loathe to have me sleep on the floor while he and Tom took the only bunk, and it was only after much expostulating that he gave his consent.

At last the night ended and daylight came. I heard a foot slipping over the edge of the bunk and thought Mr. James might have forgotten I was on the floor. "Watch out for my head," I called up to him. Carefully he threaded his way to the stove, stoked the fire, stuck his head out to feel the weather, came back, and crawled into his berth. "She still blows. We cannot move," he informed me; then once again rhythmic snores echoed through the cabin.

My cramped position during the night, the motion of the boat, the odors, and the dampness made me stiff and seasick. I gave Mr. Gadly his breakfast and made him as comfortable as possible. From experience I knew that nothing but food would relieve that empty, retching feeling in my stomach but, being Scotch, I disliked to waste our good and treasured food. However, in desperation, I finally was willing to sacrifice it. My breakfast acted as a stomach lavage. No sooner was it down than it was up and I felt like a new person. After another hearty breakfast, I was ready for anything. I must confess there swept over me an intense longing for city conveniences or even the black veil of privacy on the open deck.

All forenoon we huddled in our swaying, dripping, cozy, but wet shelter as the boat creaked, groaned, and rocked. Mr. Gadly dozed while Mr. James slept, but with one ear and one eye open. Tom read jokes from the *Reader's Digest* and I knitted on a sock for the Anglican guild bazaar.

At two o'clock, Mr. James, apparently sound asleep, landed on his feet and exclaimed, "She's stopped!" I never knew how he felt the storm cease and wakened at the exact moment, but a fisherman can be asleep one moment, while a blizzard rages, and wide awake the moment it stops. As suddenly as it had come up, the storm abated, the wind went down, and the sea subsided. The sea on this part of the Coast is like some women—erratic, whimsical of mood, uncertain of temper, and capable of producing furious storms without warning. Just as quickly it can become as gentle as a lamb. The men unlashed everything. Mr. James took the wheel and we were on our way. Mr. Gadly appeared brighter and a little stronger. Since he had been a seaman all his life he was not seasick so he had enjoyed his food and that gave him strength.

Just before darkness settled we reached a harbor and, because Mr. Gadly required considerable treatment, the men went ashore to sleep in order to give me more room to work. Before going, Mr. James left me wood for the stove and fresh drinking water, then casually remarked, "Here is my police whistle. If you feel the anchors giving way or the boat drifting out to sea, blow three blasts and I will row out to you."

Tired as Mr. James was, once he was asleep in a non-swaying bed, it would probably have taken a bomb to waken him. But with him on guard ashore and with the police whistle dangling about my neck, I felt perfectly safe.

Worn out from his treatment and the long trip, Mr. Gadly did not get to sleep, even with a strong sedative, until four o'clock in the morning. The harbor was rough, the boat heaved and tugged at the anchor chain, which clanged against the side of the boat and made sleep impossible for me. Once in that eerie watch the stillness was broken by a ghastly thump against the boat. Mr. Gadly drew himself up on to his elbow and whispered, "Is that Gabriel thumping on the wall? Has he come for me?"

The morning was radiantly beautiful. There was not a ripple on the clear, sparkling water which was so transparent that the images of the underbrush and rocks on the shore formed a double picture and it was hard to distinguish where the shoreline ended and the water picture commenced. A soft breeze stirred the grasses at the water's edge. Gulls silently skimmed the glassy water or balanced on one foot on the edge of the kinoos which were anchored to blocks of wood in the harbor.

Morning brought the men back on board and with them a sick woman with her newborn baby to go with us to the hospital.

We went around the point and, as if to speed us on our way, a brisk breeze sprang from nowhere. Just a week from the day the emergency call had reached the doctor, we docked at the Harrington Mission wharf. Dr. Gray greeted us there and I turned the patient over to him. Soon Mr. Gadly was in a hospital bed under the care of doctors and nurses. A great weight of responsibility rolled from my shoulders.

A few hours' break from duties and routine work always proved a great treat. When one worker visits another on the Coast, hours pass like minutes. For dinner a delicious goose, browned like a Christmas turkey, awaited us. This, after several days of boat food, was so wonderful I have not words to describe it! A tub bath and three hours of unbroken sleep in a stationary bed, minus woollies, for the first time since the previous Friday, was heavenly.

An old saying, "A daily bath is necessary for good health," may be true, yet I felt in the best of health and extremely alive without that indispensable bath. But it was refreshing and invigorating to luxuriate in the water. We ended the day with a pyjama party in the industrial worker's bedroom.

The following day was the doctor's birthday and the matron had planned a dinner party at the hospital. If the mail boat on which I was to return to Mutton Bay could get away in the afternoon, she would advance the party to noon. The mailman assured us that the western mailman would not be back in time for him to leave that afternoon. In order to have more time to visit, the matron loaned me one of her uniforms and I helped with the patients. Just as the lunch bell rang word came that the mail boat would leave for Mutton Bay in an hour. There was just time to have a hurried lunch, say good-bye to Mr. Gadly, and row across to the mail boat. With my heart at the evening dinner party and my body on the boat, we headed homeward.

A lovely Coast afternoon faded into a brilliant starlit evening. The northern lights sent great shafts of radiance leaping to the zenith where a curtain film changed from vivid green to orange as it rolled across the sky too swiftly for our eyes to follow. Lying on the deck, I watched the awe-inspiring and flaming beauty of the borealis light up the sky from east to west while mare's tail streaks danced from north to south.

This had been one of the most interesting trips I had taken and it had given me a deeper insight into the hardships involved in getting patients to a doctor. Also, it gave me a chance to learn how much voluntary boatmen will uncomplainingly suffer in order to be of service to their fellowmen.

CHRISTMAS, with the annual concert, mummers, and social festivities, slipped past and before we knew it we were into January, which proved to be an unusually busy month.

A scenic railway ride has nothing to equal the thrills of my first January dog-team trip. We broke the trail over hills, rocks, snowbanks, underbrush, stumps, and ballacaters.

When I answered one emergency call to another harbor, I thought I had an experienced driver with a well-trained team. Soon I realized that the young fisherman took pride in demonstrating the speed of his untrained puppies. They, as well as he, used their brawn rather than their brains. Holding my breath, I gripped the komatic and trusted to Providence. Sam, one of those illiterate, redheaded, bulldog stubborn young lads with very low mentality, was at the helm. If I said anything he would only become more reckless.

The hubbly bumps and snow-covered, icy rocks had not been smoothed down by the continuous padding of dog paws and komatics. The dogs bolted down the first steep pitch and missed, by a hair's breadth, a sharp protruding stump. Had we hit it at the rate the dogs were travelling, nothing short of a miracle would have saved us from instant death. Heedless of near danger, Sam urged the dogs to go faster. At full speed we raced down the next hill and jumped, rather than rode, across the chasm at the bottom of it, missing by a few inches a treacherous, stony gorge. Fortunately, the komatic kept level and leaped this gorge. Had the front runners dipped half an inch into the far bank, we would have been sent flying headlong five feet down among the rocks at the bottom.

As we missed treacherous, snow-covered stumps and skimmed over hazardous gorges, I became really frightened. Many lives might depend on my keeping well and healthy during the winter since there was no other nurse, doctor, or hospital available and no means of transport until May or June.

Six inches from an open, dangerous glade we just missed a huge ballacater, then catapulted onto the risky ice. I held my breath, but the ice held.

At the end of this trail two children with pneumonia presented a problem. They were too sick to move to the Station, and the home was too small to accommodate a nurse. One was very sick and the other, I thought, would readily respond to treatment. Their mother, Mrs. Brow, previously a maid in a Grenfell Mission hospital, could follow my orders, watch for dangerous symptoms, and was fairly reliable. I issued medicines, showed Mrs. Brow how to care for the children, cautioned the parents not to take chances and to let me know immediately should the children fail to recover with the prescribed treatment.

As I walked out of the house I did not look forward to that homeward trip, but the dogs had worn off some of their superfluous energy and the driver, disappointed because I had not appeared frightened and had not expostulated with him to be more careful, had lost some of his smartness. He allowed the dogs to take their time. I still felt the effects of our earlier flying ride, gripped the sides of the komatic firmly, and with a prayer for safety, kept a sharp lookout ahead for sudden, lurking dangers.

On the 15th of January I was called to a village six miles away. I examined the patient, prescribed for him, and made him comfortable. Then I set out on a round of calls, for when a nurse is called to a village she visits most of the homes. The doctor gets there once or twice a year for major repairs and treatments, so the nurse has to do the minor things. I had started through the village when an elderly man came to the door and beckoned to me. I went in and sat down. The woman and her husband drew up their chairs and started asking for news. No one appeared sick, so I waited, since I knew in due time I should be told what the trouble was.

At last Mr. Byrne hitched his chair a little closer to me, fidgeted, looked embarrassed, then leaned over and whispered, "Herns too modest. Hern willn't tell yous why hern called yous in." It was difficult for me to conceive that this brawny man, with his muscular body and deep masculine voice, could be so embarrassed. He spat into his tin cuspidor, twisted some tobacco between his fingers, placed it inside one cheek to fortify his courage, leaned closer, and again whispered. "For months hern has not been able to wear hern's shoe because hern's big toenail is so long and hard it is making hern's toe sore. I knows you can't do nothing, but will yous look at it?"

Again I wondered at this powerful-looking fisherman unable to master such a small matter as a toenail. If it had been his own, he would have ended the trouble long ago with a chisel, hammer, or saw.

Mrs. Byrne removed her stocking and I saw something like a rhinoceros' tusk! It was going to require a major operation. On paper I cannot do justice to that nail. It resembled a weather-worn, brittle, grandfather oyster shell. The next toe had an ugly sore caused by constant friction with the gnarled nail. No bandage scissors would be strong enough to tackle it. No ordinary nail file would stand the strain. I scratched my head and tried to recall operating room days. In my surgical training I had never seen anything like this nail. Mrs. Byrne must have suffered untold torture for months. I had to do something. Then suddenly I remembered watching my brothers file saws. I turned to her husband and asked, "Have you a saw file?"

"Sure," he replied, and went to the shed and brought in a twelve-inch file. For three quarters of an hour I filed and trimmed. As the nail grew smaller and thinner, her wrinkled old face beamed and she exclaimed, "John, why didn't wese think of that months ago?"

After a final trim she walked about without any pain. She

insisted that I had earned some of her best seal meat sandwiches. To her, what could be better pay?

Several weeks later one of her neighbors called at the Station to deliver this message: "Tell Sister Ise never has no more toe trouble and Ise wears my shoe all day."

February was a month for new babies and brought a variety of experience; there is no monotony in a nurse's life on the Coast.

At three o'clock on a cold morning early in the month a loud banging woke me. In answer to my shout, "What's wanted?" a man's voice replied, "Sister's in a bad way. Ise come for yous." When a fisherman says "a bad way" he means it.

When I stepped out into the inky blackness I could barely distinguish the leader dogs. The driver, Mr. Gram, seemed to sense the trail as the two of us crouched on the komatic box and sped through the darkness. Only the padding of the soft paws on the beaten trail broke the silence. When we passed under the swishing, snowladen low boughs of stunted trees which stood like ghostly phantoms beside our trail, light snow avalanched down our necks. So quiet was the night it seemed as though some Majestic Being was saying, "Hush! Be still!" Something deep in my soul was in communion with this stillness as we raced on over rocks and through underbrush. As if guided by a compass, the sure-footed dogs never faltered. Once only, when a white cottontail rabbit suddenly hopped across the trail, the leader dog swerved aside, slacked his trace, and uttered excited yelps; but in a second, loyal to duty, he was back on the trail. Before we reached a steep hill Mr. Gram removed his chain drag from his shoulder and held it ready for instant use should something or someone suddenly confront us out of the darkness.

The trail led to an open space at the top of a terribly steep hill. Barely visible in the blue-black darkness at the foot of the hill nestled a tiny home on the very brink of the sea. Only a faint glimmer of light from the coal oil lamp shone through the thickly frosted window panes. No matter how poor the family may be, there is a welcome waiting the traveller in the home behind that light. At this time of the morning, the light always spoke of trouble and anxiety for the family.

Like a toboggan, we shot down the slope and came to a halt at the doorstep in the midst of several sleeping dogs. Bristling and growling at being so roughly roused, each dog pointed his nose skyward and the cove echoed with wild wolf choruses. The anxious face of a man immediately appeared in the door. He stepped forward and shouted, "Down, down!" then, to me, "Theyse will not touch yous. Oh, Sister, Ise glad yous got here. Herns in pretty bad shape."

Mrs. Gram had had an unusually heavy day. In a few months, if everything had gone as nature intended, she would have presented her husband with another offspring to add to their already large brood. She would have had a few days holiday in bed (annually here), before picking up the routine work. Suddenly premature labor defeated nature's course.

I had already nursed in this home and, as I stepped through the low door, I recognized the room. The lowness of the ceiling on one side was exaggerated by the rough beams which supported it and left barely room to move about. Except for a fresh covering of old newspapers and pages from a mail order catalog which covered the otherwise bare wooden wall, the room had not changed. These papers do double duty—they keep out the winter blasts and help to pass the time on long stormy days and shut-in Sundays. Reading material, especially with pictures, is very scarce, and these papers provided abundant entertainment—thefts, sports, murders, fashions, and everyday events—although mostly long out of date.

There was no time to speculate on what awaited me. Mrs. Gram lay in her big double bed in the corner, the dim light shining on her ghastly white face. Weighing over two hundred pounds, she was sunk deep into the goose-feather tick and had been bleeding for several hours. The wide bed was jammed against the wall, leaving practically no floor space, so I had to crawl onto the foot of the bed and set to work. Once again I longed for a clean, hard, operating table. But by now I knew that most difficulties may be overcome. In a very short time the immediate danger was over and Mrs. Gram rested between fresh blankets.

With the first rays of dawn the eldest girl, ten years old, came downstairs and set out some food. Mr. Gram, who possessed the ingenuity and initiative necessary for the whole household, cleaned up the place. He took off a storm window so that his wife could have a little light and occasionally a breath of fresh air, then carried a substantial breakfast to her, wakened the baby, dressed and fed him, and the home settled down once more to its customary routine.

I had the day before me, so I decided to visit the homes of the village. Someone always needed sympathy or treatment. Examinations necessarily have to be of a primitive nature, but the consolation they bring is well worth the effort. A jumping tooth or a "rizin" finger may be the means of cementing confidence and friendship.

In each home, I sat and talked with the family while they asked the questions and enquired about relatives along the Coast. Or, in a tactful way, I found out about their aches and pains, colds, bad teeth, and poisonous tonsils. Many times I was able to discover whether or not a parent believed in vaccination or inoculation, which was part of my duties, or whether he considered it a lot of tommyrot.

Our consulting and examining room might be a bedchamber, a kitchen, or a pantry. At times any one of these rooms had to be turned into a chapel if the clergyman came or a morgue if there were a death. Also, any one of them might be the last resting place for frozen seals before the skinning could be done.

I encouraged mothers as I praised their children or warned them what would happen if they did not attend to minor illness or running sores. I looked at tonsils, weighed babies, painted throats, and gave aspirins and castor oil for real or imaginary troubles. Darkness fell before I had finished visiting and I decided to remain another night in order to give the rest of the children a check-up in the morning.

When bedtime came I began to wonder whether I had made a wise decision. Outside, the sparkling aurora borealis arched the sky. It was a magnificent sight, but often a forewarner of "a spell of weather" which might keep me stranded here for days or weeks. But it was too late to return home and I was too tired to lose much sleep.

During the night it turned bitterly cold. My morning toilet was a sketchy business. Shivering with cold, I dashed the icy water over my face to fortify me for what was ahead. Quickly I finished the examinations just as big, feathery flakes drifted through the air, coming down like gentle doves to warn us what we might expect before night.

Snow and ice faced us all the way to the Station. When I reached home my nose was numb and my eyelashes were frozen together so that I could not see through them. I stumbled up the Station steps into the warm kitchen. A Labrador blizzard raged for three days.

In more ways than one March came in like a lion. After the blizzard a dazzling sun shone and beehive activity spread like an epidemic.

One quiet morning the kitchen door burst open and an excited teen-age girl shouted, "The baby is here! Mum says to come quickly."

I had expected this call, but not so soon. Lily was already dashing out again as I called, "Wait, take my bag and put it on the komatic. It will take both of us to draw it on this ice."

She grabbed my maternity kit, which always stood ready for instant action, while I gathered together some baby clothes. Mary hauled on my skin boots, while I tugged a heavy windbreaker over my head. Lily and I, skidding and slipping, tugged the komatic across the tickle. The faster we tried to hurry, the more we skidded and the more time we lost. Eventually we reached the opposite side and climbed up the steep bank.

Excitement prevailed everywhere, except with young Jane, who was squatting on the floor and did not appear unduly upset. Her mother-in-law, Mrs. Montle, stood wringing her hands as Mrs. Wells, her neighbor, bent over Jane. I assured

Mrs. Montle that everything would be all right, hoping, as I set to work, that my assurance would be justified.

When he was disentangled from his mother's clothes the new arrival's howls turned to shrieks. The welcome noise made by these healthy lungs told me that I had not raised false hopes.

It took only a few seconds to cut the cord and extract the baby. Calmly Jane climbed into her waiting bed. This was her first baby and she would enjoy a few days' rest before continuing her daily work.

Jane made a remarkable recovery, to the great surprise of her neighbors, whose extremely superstitious minds had predicted a very hard time and all types of abnormalities because, wishing to earn a few extra cents, she had hooked rugs during the last days of her pregnancy. Crestfallen and probably a little disappointed, the neighbors had to admit that occasionally superstitions did not run true to tradition.

Jane settled in bed, looked about, and in a bewildered tone asked, "Is that all there is to having a baby?" Then she told me she had put on her wash water a couple of hours before with the intention of doing her weekly washing. When the water was hot, she did not feel equal to the task, so she had walked into the sitting room. In a few moments, her mother-in-law heard the baby cry and rushed for Mrs. Wells.

One night a year later this baby boy went to sleep and wakened at one o'clock to find a baby sister beside him. His sister had arrived in the world as quickly as he had, but, fortunately, this time the baby made her debut in the night and avoided undue commotion since Jane did not have to climb into bed afterward.

On the fourteenth of March, a boy rushed over with a wire. "Patient on way to Station. Doctor coming down to operate," it said.

Always the doctor did the diagnosing and notified me direct. This message baffled me because I knew the doctor was on a western trip and the wire had come from the east. All I could be sure of was that something had happened and someone was coming from somewhere with something that someone had diagnosed as needing an operation.

We filled our kettles with hot water, made a roaring kitchen fire, and set to work to scrub our tiny emergency operating room. To my knowledge there had never been a major operation performed in the Station because we did not have sterile goods nor surgical equipment for such work.

An hour later, the same boy came back with another wire. "Patient on way to Station from east, too sick to continue to hospital. Nurse and I leaving at once." This telegram explained everything, for it was from the doctor and should have been delivered before the first wire.

Such telegraphic news is public property and soon the village was turned into small, excited, expectant groups asking, "Who could it be?" "Where did the message come from?" "I wonder if he be a relative?" Then came head shakes and long sighs, with unfavorable prognosis and sympathy for the yet unknown victim.

We turned everything inside out, disinfected the entire office, and cleaned every nook and corner; then I sterilized what instruments I had. Speculation as to the nature of the case created interest even at the Station. Mary wondered if it might be a relative; she must do her best to have everything ready for her.

At five o'clock at night, as we were carrying out our last bucket of scrub water, came the yapping and howling of dogs, then two dog-teams raced down the trail. Mutton Bay dogs picked up the chorus.

When strange dogs draw near a village, for some unknown reason, dogs start howling and the village dogs answer by pointing their noses heavenward and giving long-drawn-out wolf-howls.

Men, women, and children poured out of every home to see what was coming. Two teams with eight dogs each, one with a patient and driver, and the other with the driver and the patient's sister, drove up to the Station door from the east. Yelping and jumping about in their harnesses and traces, getting tangled up, dogs and drivers snarled together as the drivers shouted commands. The commotion made our yard resemble an animal circus let loose.

Before we had the patient inside, two more teams from the west, with as many more dogs, drove up, bringing the doctor, his paraphernalia, and the nurse with her driver.

Thirty-two dogs in a snarling mix-up did not act as a sedative to a frightened, crying teen-age girl who had never been inside a hospital.

When the doctor and nurse had unloaded their komatics, we had to stumble over or thread our way among blankets and drivers' feet.

One stooped, weather-beaten, surly fisherman, who looked too tough for any germ to attack, chuckled to himself, rolled his tobacco from his lower to his upper lip, spat out the shed door, and muttered, "Huh, all this commotion for an appendix!"

When we got Bella undressed and in bed she did not appear to me to be suffering sufficiently after such a long, cold trip to indicate emergency appendicitis. In less than an hour our microscope proved the diagnosis to be incorrect. It was a medical condition and could be treated without an operation.

Mr. Butler again spat out the door, reached for his gnarled cane, and hobbled to the door, still muttering to himself, "A lot of commotion for a mere kidney. Pretty costly kidney. Ise glad hern ain't mine." I don't know whether he meant the kidney or the girl.

Little did the organization that donated that microscope know how valuable it would prove and how much suffering it saved that child. Without it we would have hesitated to take a chance and not operate, especially in this isolated district, because had it been appendicitis, another attack would probably have occurred when she was not within reach of the doctor.

Much more unnecessary suffering and expense might be saved could we have modern equipment at strategic points along the Coast.

All this excitement deserved the best we had. The doctor, nurse, and I had some choice lobster, which we kept for special occasions, and then we settled by the fireplace for a well-earned lazy evening. In the morning, the doctor packed their equipment onto the komatics and left for home. In less than a week Bella drove away with her appendix intact.

A nurse must see the humorous, as well as the tragic side of her work. She must be hardened, but not hard, or she will break. Neurosis, lonesomeness, or Coast sickness will break her unless she can have a good laugh in the midst of tragedy.

When tragedy strikes, nature balances the sanity of the human race by presenting at the same time the humorous side of the picture.

One day when I was returning home extremely depressed from witnessing a terrible tragedy, we came to a little village and I saw a woman across the tickle, standing at her back door frantically waving her hands and shouting to us. My heart sank. Another tragedy, I thought, will finish me. Bill stopped the dogs so that we could hear what she was shouting. She cupped her hands to her mouth and I strained my ears. On the wind I caught the words, "Has yous a souse with yous?"

I shouted back, "A what?"

Again the wind brought, "Has yous a souse?"

"What do you want to do with it?" Sometimes if I could learn what people did with an article I could figure out what was needed. Before her answer came back I noticed the driver nearly doubled with laughter. When he saw my bewilderment he stopped laughing sufficiently to say, "She means one of those rubber things you stick in a baby's mouth when you give him the bottle. Yous knows because yous gave me one for Albert last week." Enlightened, I shouted back, "I have none with me, but I will send you one the first chance I have."

"All right," she shouted, "Ise'll send yous a nickel the first time someone goes up."

I had a good laugh as Bill started the dogs and we continued on our way. Never had I thought a rubber nipple could provide sufficient relaxation to avert nervous tension so completely.

Since November I had walked, skidded, and mushed with my toes behind komatics so much that by the end of March water soaked through the soles and toes of my boots. The legs were good so Mrs. Tole agreed to put new feet on them. But, said she, "Theyse are green so Ise'll has to soak theyse overnight before Ise can sew theyse. Theyse will not be ready for a couple of days."

In olden days women used to chew them (I believe the Eskimo women still do) instead of soaking them. What a taste that would be!

The next afternoon I was walking by Mrs. Tole's place wearing moccasins instead of sealskin boots. I heard a small voice pipe up, "Mum has your boots finished but theyse'll not be dry until tomorrow." It was Mrs. Tole's four-year-old boy. It struck me as remarkable that a child of his age should notice my moccasins and connect them with the sealskin boots. But I need not have been surprised; Coast people are constantly watching for changes in the weather and they are quick to notice a change in clothing.

Frequently I was asked, "How much did you pay for it?" "Where did you get it?" and "Is it new?" If one dons a new garment everyone wants to know all about it. Not idle curiosity but friendly interest prompts them to ask such questions. It is much more of an event to buy a new dress or coat, furniture or dish, than it is to have a baby. By the time a woman feels justified in buying anything new her old clothes have been seen, studied, and known for months or years. Many women can tell just how many dots or stripes there are in a certain piece of cloth.

Coast children, and more especially young women, have a remarkable ability to memorize page after page of poetry or prose. Because they have had to make their own social life, furnish their own entertainments, and stage their own dramatic plays they have developed marvellous memories.

To take part in a dialogue, one young girl memorized twenty-one pages of prose in a few days. She did not have much education and many of the words had never been used in her presence, nor had she seen them in print until she started to memorize her part.

One lad, who had never been inside a schoolhouse to study, was needed for a play. Finally we coaxed him to take part. Someone read him the words so that he could memorize them. When he took his place on the platform it was impossible to separate his acting from that of those who had been able to read their parts. This remarkable power of memorizing may be due, in part, to the fact that schools were (and still are) few and far between. Many of the older people and some of the younger ones never had the opportunity to learn to read or write, so they depend entirely on their memories.

February and March had been all work and no play. April, with its long, sunny days and crisp, frosty nights brought new life and energy to everyone. An urge to do something besides my regular nursing possessed me. All the immediately expected babies had arrived, diarrhea epidemics had somewhat subsided, and my two pneumonia cases were out of bed. Yet nothing seemed to go right with me. I knew that if I could have a short break away from stoking, supervising, and sickness, life would be more like living than just existing. The break came more quickly than I expected. Late one night I was visiting a sick child when I heard Mr. Orman say that he was going trout fishing the next morning. The snow crust was ideal for travelling and the wind had swept the snow off the ice. Ice fishing was done by cutting holes in the ice so that the trout see daylight and think spring has come. They swim to the holes and leap up for the bait. I love fishing so I asked, "How would you like a passenger?" "Sure," he replied, "but yous'll have to be ready at daylight (four o'clock) as wese have to travel on the crust."

At the mention of a fishing trip my weariness dropped from me. I had heard so much about trout fishing through the ice that I felt it would be a fine relaxation. I went home and laid out my heavy clothes, fishing line, hooks, and a piece of salt pork for bait.

At three-thirty in the morning my alarm jangled. I lighted the kerosene lamp, raised myself onto my elbow, and looked out. The weather was with us. It was a perfect morning, nippy with not too much wind; daylight lurked behind a thin, dark cloud. Muffled to the chin, I went downstairs and rustled up a cup of hot chocolate, a hunk of bread and cheese, and a bowl of cornflakes. As I finished eating, far out across the tickle I could distinguish a black dog-team mushing in our direction. Soon Mr. Orman and his little son, Billy, halted the team. I jumped onto the komatic box behind them, feeling like a Teddy bear in my sweaters, mitts, and dickie.

At this time of year starting on a fishing trip at daybreak provides more thrills than an ordinary boat fishing trip. Silently and quickly we sped over the crisp snow and ice and soon left Mutton Bay and the tickle far behind. We climbed up the rocky hills and when we reached the top of the first peak day broke all about us. The sun threw pale pink, then bright red streaks over the treetops. There was a crackling sensation in the air and the crust sparkled like diamonds and crunched under the dogs' paws. The dogs raced up the hills, around ballacaters, across frozen ponds, then dipped into the valleys between cliffs. Excitedly they scrambled up rocky cliffs, pushed their way through tangled underbrush, and then swung out on the long level stretch of portage. Here they loped into a swift gait which made the komatic slew from side to side on the glassy crust.

Three miles out we caught up with Mr. Whitney and his son, who were heading for the same river. They knew we were coming and since they did not know the way "in river" they were waiting to follow us. For a while, side by side, neck and neck, the teams strove to keep ahead of each other. Soon we left the others behind because they had young puppies which could not travel as fast as our experienced dogs; also, their driver was a young lad just learning the art of handling dogs.

When we came to the trout river, fourteen miles inland, it was evident that fishermen had been there the previous day because we found several holes through the thick ice and fir boughs, on which they had knelt while fishing, near by.

Mr. Orman, an old-timer, knew all the tricks of ice fishing. Immediately he set to work drilling more holes where he suspected good fishing. He had fastened a sharp-bladed chisel at the end of a long, round pole and, with the sharp edge pressed hard against the ice, he twirled the handle back and forth between his mittened hands until it broke through the ice to the water below.

We baited our hooks with salt pork, chose what we thought would be the best holes, and dropped in our hooks, sinkers, and lines, then knelt on the boughs and jigged our lines up and down. Billy soon pulled up a twelve-inch trout. After that we jigged hard and furiously but caught only small tommycods and gasperos.

At twelve o'clock Mr. Orman exclaimed, "Time to eat. There

will be no more fish for an hour. Let's eat and be ready for them when they start to run again." He knew that trout feed at certain intervals, then have a siesta.

Except for cold, damp knees and small fry, we did not have much to show for our forenoon's sport. But I had worked up a gnawing appetite and was completely relaxed and felt like a new person. Miles from sick people, yet knowing they could reach me if an emergency arose, I felt gloriously free.

We tethered the dogs so that they would not run home, then pulled our komatics into the shelter of the bush near the trees. Mr. Orman stuck some posts into a deep bank, laid on a few twigs which he gathered from the bushes, and touched a match to them. In a few moments we had a blazing fire over which we hung a lard pail with a wire handle. When it boiled, Mr. Orman threw in a handful of black tea and two dry twigs to settle the ashes. After it had boiled fifteen minutes he pronounced it ready to drink. I set up a makeshift table on one of the komatic boxes and made brush cushions. Billy sat on the brush, Mr. Whitney and Donald knelt on one komatic, and Mr. Orman and I on a box. He served the baked beans while I passed around cheese, canned sausage, bread, and cookies. There were dozens of cinders in the canned beans, the tea was strong enough to float an egg, and the canned sausages were half cold and greasy, but I enjoyed every mouthful and ate more than I had eaten at one meal for the past three weeks.

We washed the dishes in snow, packed them away, tucked the leftover food into papers, and went back to the ice. As Mr. Orman had predicted, the fish had finished their siesta and had started to run again. In quick succession we flicked tommycod and gasperos from the holes. Three other trout, which were beauties, flashed through the air and were flung far out on the ice, but luck was not with me that day. I did not land a single trout. After nearly an hour a lull came. Mr. Orman exclaimed, "Fish are like us. They works by spells and they eats by spells. Theyse will rest now so we might as well go home."

We had a mug-up of leftover food, packed our things, and started home. Like a great red ball, the sun crept away behind the hills and left a purple-red glow stretched across the sky as it slowly sank out of sight below the horizon. Tired, happy, relaxed, and satisfied, I enjoyed every moment as we mushed over the hills and ice. And what a good supper we had!

It was not as much fun cleaning and preparing the fish as it had been flashing them out of the water, but I shall never forget the delicious flavor of those crackly well-browned beauties.

DURING the latter part of April the ice began to break in places, but I had one more interesting dog-team trip before it gave way. When the ice in Labrador starts to catch in the fall and begins to break in the spring, we travel by dog-team-canoe—when travel is possible at all.

I received a wire begging me, "Come somehow."

When Jack brought the message he assured me that it would be "somehow."

I had heard them talking about taking a kinoo on the dog-teams, but I did not realize all that was involved in such a trip.

Jack looked in the door and added, "Ise will be back for yous in half an hour. Yous had better wear rubber boots." This seemed strange because we always wore sealskin boots at this time of year on dog-team trips.

In less than half an hour Jack arrived with a large kinoo on the komatic. When I went down the Station steps he shouted, "Jump into the kinoo." I jumped in and the dogs dashed up the hill. For the first mile we mushed silently over ice and snow, under the blue sky with vast open space on all sides. I wished that all the people who must hustle and bustle about a city might take a year or two from their busy lives and share it with these simple people. In body, mind, and soul they would return home refreshed and strengthened. Here, man seemed made to live, the world made for him and not man for the world.

My daydreams ended abruptly. Without warning, from a fast trot the dogs stopped dead still on the brink of a yawning gap of open water. Jack shouted back, "Sit still and Ise'll row yous across." He unhitched the dogs and they, without hesitation, leaped into the icy salt water and swam to the other side, their traces trailing behind. They shook the dripping water from their long, furry coats while Jack pushed our kinoo into the open glade, rowed across, then pulled the kinoo onto the ice on the opposite side. Before we reached our destination, we had to repeat this two-way travel four times. I began to realize what "Get there somehow" meant. Many times this use of dog-teams is the only way the mailman can get through with his mail. When he feels, in his bones, that the ice is going to break up, he engages a dozen or more teams to rush mail over the ice.

This particular trip was a difficult one, but well worth while, for I was able to relieve a patient in agonizing pain, and leave medicines for preventing or relieving future attacks.

Like the mailman I could feel spring tingling in my blood and knew it was time to house clean. We had postponed the cleaning as long as possible so that every conceivable emergency might be over. One lovely May morning we packed the upstairs furniture into the ward so that the women might scrub the upstairs. They were not quite finished when they went home for the night, planning to continue early next morning.

At seven o'clock Nora, a young expectant mother with dangerously puffed cheeks, swollen eyelids, stovepipe shiny legs and ankles walked into my office and exclaimed, "Ise feels sick." She complained of seeing black specks before her eyes but she was not worried because she did not expect her baby for another month. The moment I saw her, I knew that the month might be minutes or hours. Her husband would not be home for several weeks, so I sent for her mother-in-law, Mrs. Greg, with whom she lived, and explained that the girl was seriously ill, that she might take convulsions at any moment, and might not live through the confinement. I advised her to wire for, or take Nora to, a doctor immediately. Mrs. Greg took my wire to the operator and soon a message came from the doctor: "Impossible to travel with patient in that condition. No boat can get through with me as the harbors are jammed with ice."

There was nothing to do but face the situation with Mrs. Greg to assist me.

After hovering between life and death for two days and nights, Nora had the expected convulsions and a tiny baby boy was born. He breathed and that was about all. Nora was in a severe convulsion and it was not safe to leave her, so I passed the baby to Mrs. Greg and instructed her to wrap it in absorbent cotton and put it in a box on the oven door in the kitchen. She went down with the baby, but before she had time to get it properly wrapped, Nora had another more severe convulsion and a second wee boy came into the world. Mrs. Greg wrapped this baby in cotton and placed him beside his brother. I did not expect either of the babies to live and considered the mother's life in danger, so I remained with her. Two hours later I could go downstairs and was surprised to find both babies giving signs of being very much alive. I dragged in our general purpose boiler and made an improvised incubator with irons, hot-water bottles, and pillows. This incubator on the oven door was the twins' first bed.

A few weeks before, Nora's cousin had been confined and I knew that nature had supplied her with sufficient milk to feed two babies. I rushed a note to her and asked her to spare some of her milk for the twins. Her sister came running to the Station with the precious milk, which I dropped into the tiny mouths every two hours night and day. With this co-operative feeding, the babies began to grow, and soon their cries sounded like normal babies' howls. When Nora was strong enough to be moved home, she had to be rowed across the tickle. The twins were so tiny I was afraid of losing them overboard, so I wrapped them in blankets, papoose fashion, and tied them to the top of an orange crate. Sleeping safely and snugly on these boards balanced across my knees, they were rowed home with their proud mother.

June brought boat travel and summer life began in earnest. I had made some puppets and was trying to interest the teen-age girls in making them for a show to raise some money for the church. I hung up one of my puppets in the kitchen-waiting room. The first day several callers admired my puppets, asked questions, and wanted me to explain how they worked. I made Hansel and Gretel walk, dance, and jump about. One man became so interested he forgot his errand and went home with his wife's note in his pocket; later his daughter had to come back with the note. The second day I was swamped with real or imaginary errands and the puppets performed all afternoon.

At seven o'clock that evening, we lighted the lamp. The full moon shed its rays on the rocks but our shed was pitch dark. I was standing on a chair pulling Hansel's strings while several small girls hopped about with delight when suddenly three huge, swarthy men with long, black, piratelike beards passed by the window. They knocked loudly and I had to go into the dark shed to answer the door. The day before we had been notified by the Seven Islands police to report immediately if we saw any suspicious person, any strange piece of driftwood or anything that might pertain to a foreign boat in our vicinity. Submarines were near us and every precaution had to be taken.

As soon as I saw these men pass the window, I recalled the picture of a black-bearded, burly German that I had seen in a newspaper. There was not a man at the Station. With fear and trepidation, I saw them enter the kitchen. When the children saw the strange faces they huddled behind the stove. Boldly, but inwardly quaking, I asked, "What do you want?" The largest one replied in a gruff voice, "We have a man on board our ship who needs nursing care and we have come for you."

I shivered with fear. That was exactly what the papers recently had published. "Men from an enemy vessel will come ashore asking for a doctor or nurse to go aboard. They will glide in unnoticed and then sail away with the person for questioning."

The paper went on to relate how "they" would brutally torture the person until he or she gave them the desired information. Tonight that victim would be me. As a rule, on the Coast, one does not think quickly but ponders and meditates. But this was an extreme emergency and I thought and acted quickly.

I said firmly to the burly sailor, "Come into my office until I discuss the matter with you." They all went ahead of me, so I turned to Mary and whispered, "Run to the telegraph office and find out who these men are. Get a man to come back with you if they are not known."

Stalling for time until Mary could return, I began questioning them. They stated they had been sent ashore by the captain to get me after one of the sailors had gone out of his mind. They had him tied in the hold, but everyone was afraid to go near him so they wanted me to come aboard and take care of him. They had come for morphine or something to keep him quiet until they could reach some harbor, where they could take him ashore and send him home by plane. All of this fitted in with the warnings I had read in the papers. It must be a German vessel . . . a submarine perhaps! We had not heard any unfamiliar motor come into the harbor.

While I was still questioning them about the deranged sailor, Mary returned. The operator had said these men had come ashore from one of our regular Government boats which brought the annual supplies to the lighthouse keepers along the Atlantic coast. I relaxed and rebuked my imagination. Gladly would I do anything to help the suffering man, but first I would have to wire the doctor for permission to use morphine. On the way to the boat I sent a wire and the doctor gave his consent.

We rowed out to the vessel and I gave the man a hypodermic,

remaining with him until he dropped off to sleep. It was not necessary for me to stay with him, but the captain wanted me to remain on board the rest of the night. I discovered that there were thirty men on the ship. I would be the only woman. Since it was two o'clock in the morning and I would have to work all the next day, the Marconi operator invited me to take his berth for the remaining few hours and said he would bunk with one of the crew. Without a thought of fear, with unlocked door, I crawled into the berth and rested until daylight. Those rough, hardy sailors, drawn together by a common cause—helping the mental agony of one man—showed me the greatest respect and courtesy.

In the morning I had breakfast with Captain Mack and it was well worth losing a night's sleep for that meal. Grapefruit, ham, eggs, toast, and jam—to me it was a banquet. I examined the patient, then two sailors rowed me ashore.

I am very fond of the game of monopoly, and one lovely June evening I had been invited to the parsonage for a game. Dressed in my Sunday and only good dress, I went across anticipating an enjoyable evening. As I unfastened my coat a child ran up the steps shouting, "She's coming in. A strange boat is unloading a sick baby at the Station wharf."

It was a Newfoundland boat bringing Miss Bright, our Mission nurse from Forteau. She was supposed to take her patients across the Strait to St. Anthony, Newfoundland. However, the ice blocked travel across the Strait so the custom's officer had given her permission to bring this presumably dying child into Canada to the only doctor available. Crouched under a canvas shelter in an open boat most of the night and all day, she had travelled through rough water, dodging ice floes and shoals, in order to reach Mutton Bay before night. From outward appearance the baby might be dead, and both were exhausted. It was too late to try to reach the hospital that night so we carried little Peter into my Station.

After a hot supper Miss Bright went to bed and I stayed with Peter until three o'clock in the morning. When it was light enough to see the rocks the men carried Peter out to the boat and they set off for the hospital at Harrington Harbour. Peter had to have a constant icecap. Along the way they had stopped frequently and broken off pieces of ice floe to refill the cap. Fortunately, a benefactor had donated a coal oil refrigerator to the Mutton Bay Station, so we were able to fill his icecap with cubes, which lasted until he reached the hospital.

I never expected to see Peter alive again but most children are like cats and have nine lives. A few weeks later, rosy and happy as he played about the deck, Peter rode home in state on the Mission boat.

Besides being a nurse it is necessary to be a cook, for sometimes the maid problem is rather complicated. When war called away many men, extra hands were needed at the canneries so maids were scarce and inexperienced. Most of them were young and had never cooked from recipes. Heat, flies, and training a new maid gave me a few more grey hairs and taxed my nerves and stomach to the limit.

I had to stand with Jane and explain the difference between a half and a quarter. What did it matter whether one used a teaspoon or a tablespoon? When blancmange, looking like leather and requiring a knife to cut it, was served, I knew that Jane had refused to use measurements. She persisted in using handfuls and guesswork. "My mother herns just guesses," she replied every time I tried to teach her. Oatmeal or farina, made from the same recipe, might appear in the form of gruel or heaped-up dough. Once I asked her how much cornstarch the pudding recipe required and she replied, "Ise sure Ise don't knows. Ise never bothers with those cookbooks. Ise just puts in a handful." It tasted like a good-sized handful.

One day a cake, which required a tablespoon of soda, appeared on the table looking like a wrinkled brown lemon. I went out and asked Jane what spoon she had used. She showed me the bread spoon. Disgusted, I exclaimed, "But Jane, I have told you time and again that a tablespoon is the next size larger than the spoon we use for our cereal. Why did you use this one?" "It was in the table drawer so I thought it was a tablespoon," she replied innocently. What was a little soda, more or less, in her life? She had never seen it before she came to the Station.

I enjoy nicely cooked food but I soon learned not to be too particular. It was never wise to look at things too closely or to analyze the contents. As long as it was nourishing and had been boiled or baked it would not kill me and it was food.

As everywhere, on the Coast babies come and have to be baptized, weddings take place, men die, and funerals are held. As the nurse, I participated in all three occasions. Unless the nurse enters into the joys, sorrows, pleasures, and social life of the village, she cannot give the most efficient service.

As I have already stated, the visit of a travelling clergyman creates much excitement. On his arrival, the clergyman takes stock of what is to be done: how many services he can work in, how many holy communions for shut-ins, how many weddings are pending, how many parents have to be interviewed, and how many baptismal services he will have to perform.

The last part of July, Mr. Meek unexpectedly changed his plans and made a premature visit to Mutton Bay. Consternation and commotion ensued. Mr. Meek arrived late Saturday afternoon. Five newborn babies were to be baptized so there was a running to and fro from home to home to find suitable christening clothes. At the Station we had one complete outfit, consisting of a snow-white dress decorated with trailing blue ribbons. This was borrowed, worn, laundered, and returned ready for the next new arrival. Mr. Meek's unexpected arrival before the boat had brought material for christening clothes was a calamity.

One old-timer remarked, "An unheard of thing in this village! We never has had five at one time! What has happened to this young generation?"

After a complete combing of the village only three additional robes could be found. Four babies were to be baptized at the church, and the other, only four days old, at the Station because the mother was not able to go to the church. I assured this mother, Mrs. Ross, that our robe could do double duty. She was from another harbor and wanted her baby baptized before she left Mutton Bay because there was a Protestant-Catholic pull in her family. I asked Mr. Meek to tell the first mother to remove the dress as soon as she left the morning service and send it immediately to the Station so that we could air it for our baby. Mr. Meek obligingly agreed to do so—that is, if he did not forget. Well-meaning, the spirit willing, but apparently the flesh weak, his mind was on more important issues and this matter completely slipped his mind.

The four babies, named and cooing, were proudly carried home and inspected by multitudes of relatives.

Shortly after lunch, I saw Mr. Meek coming to the Station to baptize our baby. The borrowed dress had not been returned. When he reached the Station I surmised what had happened. Embarrassed, he admitted, "I completely forgot it." A little girl came around the corner so I sent her posthaste for the dress. Patiently Mr. Meek waited on our porch steps. Blanche came running back with the outfit. It was an extremely hot day and the dress was moist with perspiration, but we freshened it as well as we could and soon our baby was gowned, baptized, and received into the Protestant Church.

Little did the person who so kindly donated the christening outfit know how much pleasure the simple, yet so important, feminine touches on that dress brought to many a mother's heart.

ONCE more summer was forgotten and winter was upon us.

For two days and nights during December I had nursed Theresa LeGrand in her home. She was delirious with a high temperature and was gradually growing weaker. I suspected she had meningitis but had no equipment to prove my diagnosis. Also, I could not give her proper nursing care in her overcrowded home. Should a test show that it was tubercular meningitis, no nursing care would save her.

Our last steamer, before navigation closed for the winter, was at a port three miles away. There was a fifty-fifty chance for the girl's life if we could get her to a hospital on that steamer. If not, there would be no means of travel for a month or two until there was enough snow for dog-teams. Even then, it would be a terribly rough trip for a sick patient.

At nine o'clock that night her parents gave their consent. It was a hard decision to make. My heart went out to them. Perhaps she might have a chance at the hospital. At home they were watching her slowly slip away from them in excruciating pain.

The next problem was to persuade the captain to call at our port for us. With the aid of flashlights we skidded and plodded what seemed thirty, rather than three, miles over rocks, across partly frozen ice, over portages, and through underbrush to the cove where the steamer was anchored. When we reached the anchored steamer, the gangplank was drawn up and stowed away. I routed out two men who were working in the fishing stage near by and told them that it was absolutely necessary to see the captain. One of them shouted to a sailor on the black deck. No lights except flashlights could be used because we were in the black-out district. Through the darkness we could barely distinguish the sailor, but a gruff voice shouted down, "Wats wanted?" As soon as he realized it was a matter of life and death for me to interview the captain he stooped over the rail, seized my hands, and shouted down, "Heave to." I hove to and the men boosted from below. When I reached the rail he hauled me over. He kept his hand over the flashlight ray to make it as dim as possible. I stumbled behind him to the captain's office. At first he flatly refused to stop the steamer at Mutton Bay. After much persuasion he wavered, then relented and agreed to stop fifteen minutes at daybreak outside in the open water. Then he added, "I dare not call at the port on account of shore ice and if you are not ready outside I can not wait." Satisfied that he would keep his promise, I left the steamer the same way I had come. We skidded and plunged through the darkness back to the house, then located a small boat to take Theresa to the steamer.

Late into the night the men sawed and nailed boards as they made a stretcher to go into the miniature cabin-house on the boat. Women darted here and there hunting for clean, warm clothing. One woman came with a long, flowing flannellette nightgown, another brought her sleeping bag, while others carried in woollen blankets. When everything was in readiness, I left the patient with her parents, priest, and neighbors and went over the trail, a mile away, to the home of the mailman, whose sons were to take the patient to the steamer in their boat.

At five o'clock on that bleak, frosty, dark December morning, we hiked the mile over frozen bays by the rays of flashlights and waded through freshly fallen snowbanks.

Fortunately the tide was with us. The men carried the stretcher over the ice, stepped into shallow slob water and lifted it into the boat. It was impossible to get the whole stretcher under cover, so Theresa was slid in, feet first, until only her head remained protruding from the cabin door. To protect her from the biting wind, we hung a piece of canvas over the stretcher. Cozy and warm, she swayed at a precarious angle as the men held each side of the stretcher to keep it from overbalancing. We chugged by the light of a lantern through the ice out of the harbor.

Slowly we snaked our way through the choppy slob ice and water until we came to the clear water passage where the steamer had agreed to pick us up. Shortly after our arrival day began to break and we heard, far in the distance, the steamer cutting her way toward us. True to his word, the captain drew the steamer alongside of us. Instead of using the swaying accommodation ladder, the huge side of the steamer was lifted out. The crew stepped forward and our men lifted the stretcher up to those waiting above, who, in turn, lifted it to others on the next deck. They carried Theresa, on her stretcher, into the dining room and placed her on the table. With a shove from below and boost from above, Mrs. LeGrand and I were stowed safely aboard, and the steamer was again in motion.

Theresa, with her drawn white face and feverish bright black eyes surrounded by sunken, dark circles, peered up at us from her furry hood. Her life hung on a thread and I wondered whether or not that thread would break. She rallied somewhat but it was an extremely anxious time for Mrs. LeGrand. I could do very little and could offer her only doubtful comfort.

Before the steamer docked I saw the doctor, accompanied by men, waiting with a stretcher to carry Theresa to the hospital. Laboratory tests confirmed my diagnosis of tubercular meningitis. Unless a miracle happened, there was no hope. For forty-eight hours Theresa held her own and then rapidly became weaker and on Tuesday she died.

Northern winds swept the Coast. Slob ice drifted in and out making winter travel dangerous and uncertain. The mail plane was due in the harbor about the eighteenth. This might mean the eighteenth of December or it might mean the eighteenth of January. In order to reach it, we would have to go four miles by boat and two miles by dog-team. The plane could not land at Mutton Bay, so I would have to go down at the next village, six miles eastward, if the ice were "caught" enough for a plane to land. Should it not be caught, I would be stranded miles to the east. Even if it were caught, the trail was not yet passable for dogs and I would have to hike back over the hills a risky six or eight miles over unbroken, rough trail. The local mailman measured the ice and found it only eight inches thick. For a plane to land, it had to be eleven inches. No one could tell whether it would be one or five weeks before the plane could land. My Christmas work at the Station was accumulating, and I was anxious to get home. Mrs. LeGrand wanted to take the body home before travel became absolutely impossible. The next morning, after a long consultation, we decided to make an attempt to get through by open boat. At the worst, we could return to the hospital before darkness set in.

The man brought the motorboat as close to the wharf as possible, carried the casket aboard and lashed it securely to the foredeck. In borrowed heavy clothing and wrapped in blankets with hot-water bottles in our laps, we crouched in the center of the boat under a piece of canvas, where we were fairly well protected from the worst of the wind's violence.

Unfortunately the wind and slob ice worked against us. We had made only fifteen miles before darkness set in and we had to seek shelter at Mrs. LeGrand's old home, now a seal fishery used only during the sealing season. This home was the only building on that small island. We anchored and the men clawed their way up the icy bank, dragging the casket behind them. Shortly, in a corner of the pantry, a small chapel with burning candles was arranged. Night and day, at stated intervals, we gathered around the casket, knelt, and were led by a cousin through various prayers.

We had hoped to leave for my Station at daybreak, but during the night a gale bore down on us and the snowstorm which followed made travel impossible. The people in this home were very generous to us; they gave us of their best. There were nine seal fishermen, two women to do the cooking, Mrs. LeGrand, the body, and me.

Outside the blizzard roared and rampaged but the men managed to get out, between squalls, and clear the seals from their nets. I longed for a breath of fresh air but the men forbade me to set foot outside the door in such a storm. An Off-coaster, if wise, never goes against the advice of an old fisherman, especially in the face of "weather."

The only contact with the outside world was a peephole which the men made by breathing on the frosty window pane. Each time they went to look out they had to breathe on the pane and wipe away the frost.

The grandfather and Mrs. LeGrand could speak English but general conversation was carried on in French. Occasionally one of them would explain something to me or ask me a question in English.

On one side of the room a huge stove, built for long and constant usage, was surrounded, especially at night, by dozens of sealskin boots. On a line behind the stove hung a multitude of socks and mitts. The seal fishermen came in with their mittens soaked with icy salt water and dropped them into a bucket of fresh water which always stood back of the stove. Later, they were wrung out and hung up ready for the next change. The remainder of that side of the room was lined with a neat pile of split wood. Safe from the storm, a vast barrel of ice and water stood against the wall. As soon as some of the ice melted so that they could dip out water a man would go out, cut more ice, bring it in and fill the barrel. Every time he opened the door, wisps of snow and gusts of biting wind swept the dust across the floor and we could hear the force of the storm as it panted, bellowed, and raged over the sea and rocks.

The walls were hung with pictures. One photograph of a daughter who had attended school in Quebec seemed to be especially treasured and they explained how wonderful it was that she had been away to the city. On the opposite wall hung a large banjo and a small violin. Overhead, in the rafters, were five rifles and ramrods. This was a well-established, talented family. The musical instruments and the college picture spoke of the ambitions of the old French grandparents. The guns indicated the presence of hunters as well as fishermen. A fisherman has to be a hunter as well to make a success of living on the Coast. Guns are used to kill birds for food and to shoot seals far out on the ice, but are not needed for protection.

In the center of the floor was an immense trap door. When it was opened I could see huge boxes of home-cooked bread, pails of lard, salt pork, fish, salt, native berries, and other food which they had brought from their mainland home. Foresight, thrift, economy, and prosperity were apparent in this cellar. Should the first spring steamer be late in coming, these people would not have to call for relief. Necessity had taught them to store away their supplies in the fall, ready for any emergency the next spring. Always they would have something to spare for those less fortunate.

I never ceased to marvel at the many skills and ingenuity of some fishermen. When it is too stormy to fish, they can turn to some other craft. The wind fairly shrieked around the house, snow swirled about the windows, and breakers boomed against the rocks. But in one corner the grandfather, who expected to receive an old-age pension in the spring, was unconcernedly softening a dog harness by passing it over a well-worn file.

In another corner, Silas, one of the younger men, was taking the fur off a sealskin, getting it ready to make a dog harness, while another was oiling sealskin boots. At the window, Ed had two duties to perform. From this minute peephole he kept watch over the seal nets far out in the water. Whenever a seal got caught in the meshes he could see the sleek, shiny head bobbing up and down. He also kept an eye on the dogs that frequently sneaked up to steal some of the seal meat. When the seals were brought ashore they were laid side by side in rows in such a way that they would not freeze together or have their skins damaged by contact with the others. Hundreds of seals were lined up a few hundred feet from the house and they were quite a temptation for the hungry dogs.

Ed breathed through the peephole, spotted a dog, and suddenly let out a bloodcurdling shout. At first these shouts made me jump almost out of my chair. When the dogs heard the shout they knew someone was watching their movements and they curled their tails between their legs and slunk away. In a few moments they would wriggle back just in case that eagle eye might miss them. If a shout brought no results Ed would jump from his chair, make a dash out the door, and fling a chunk of wood or frozen ice at them, and there would be a medley of howling dogs scampering for safety. At night the dogs were locked into their kennels.

One daughter, who was in charge of this home during the seal-fishing season because her mother had to stay inland with another daughter who was expecting a baby, was frying dozens of bread drop doughnuts in a heavy iron pot of lard. The rest of the men lounged about, dozing and smoking.

Morning dawned clear and fine. We were anxious to make an early start and the men rigged up a canvas tent on the boat.

Once more the casket was lashed to the deck. We crawled under our canvas tent and huddled beside a pail in which a wood fire smouldered and threw out an intermittent heat. A pipe stuck through the canvas carried away part of the choking smoke.

For two hours we made our way slowly through open water and slob ice, then rounded the point in sight of Mutton Bay. But then our boat commenced to ice over and the slob began to thicken and drift rapidly. Like a mirage of travelling glass the ice advanced toward us with such speed that if it struck our boat it would shatter it to splinters. Mr. Monteau stuck his head inside our tent and exclaimed, "There is nothing to do but try and make it back home. Wes must not risk it in this ice." Much as he hated to admit defeat, he knew the dangers of the sea. Cautiously avoiding hard cakes of ice, he swung the boat through the shimmering, swaying, glassy sheets and we headed back to the seal fishery. When we arrived there, once more the body was dragged up the icy banks into the house and a few more prayers were repeated.

Our travel problem was discussed from every angle. Finally it was decided to try to make the mainland from another direction. Mr. Monteau wired the mainland and asked two men with dog-teams to be at a certain spot at a definite hour late that afternoon. If we were not at the appointed place, they were to go home, since our failure to appear would indicate that we were unable to make the trip.

Again the casket was shoved down the icy bank and lashed to the deck. About halfway to the mainland, our boat, heavily coated with ice, canted sideways. We drew in close to a small, rocky island and the men cut off the icy encasement. With the heavy weight gone, the boat righted itself, and at last we reached the appointed cove. Two men and teams, with open komatics, their backs to the wind, stamped back and forth to keep warm while they waited for us. Slowly and carefully the men poled the boat close to a large ballacater. When we were within stepping distance, they swung us over the edge and we scrambled to the shore.

At the sight of the dogs leaping and barking, new energy coursed through my veins, but we were chilled from the long boat ride and as we raced along the wind seemed to eat its way through our clothing. But it was a great relief to be on the mainland and to know that we could reach home, somehow, without having to depend on the sea. Just before we reached the village my driver casually remarked, "Yous nose is getting white." I had not felt it and after a brisk rub with my mittened hand it did not give me any trouble.

We placed the casket in an empty schoolhouse. Mrs. LeGrand went to one home and I to another. I was in the home of a Mr. Monteau, a brother of the seal fisherman in whose house we had been stranded. For many years this man had been the only Whale Head midwife. He received his old-age pension but still practised his profession. He and his wife and a grown son lived here; they welcomed us warmly, and the son, Norman, volunteered to take me by dog-team at daylight the six miles to the mailman's home.

Living their primitive life with practically no luxuries, few conveniences, and enduring severe hardships, this happy, contented couple left a deep impression on me. One act showed their genuine good manners. The family washbasin was in the corner of the combined dining room-kitchen. Before the meal, this tiny, white-haired, elderly woman combed her hair and without a word, as if from long custom, turned her back to her husband, who carefully brushed off every stray hair before she came near the table. Recently they had moved into a new house, which was far from complete, and they were having difficulty heating it sufficiently for comfort. The weather had suddenly turned bitterly cold so we huddled around the stove until bedtime. Norman, who could speak English, brought his ten-foot komatic and dog harnesses close to the stove in order to thaw the ice from the runners and to take the frostiness from the harnesses.

At daybreak, after a burr-r-ry cold dip in the washbasin, handshakes, and a "God bless you" from our kind hosts, we were off.

The previous night, I had contacted the mailman, who was to relay me the remaining fifteen miles over the hills and bays to the Station.

When we set out the sun was below the horizon but daylight was beginning to break over the treetops and there was a nip in the air. The snow had a crispness which made the runners crunch and squeak over the trail as we sped along.

The mailman's wife, Mrs. Brown, came out to greet me. I recognized her as the mother of my first Coast baby, born fifteen years before. She removed my boots and insisted that I have a hot drink before starting the next lap of the trip, then she loaned me extra blankets and her coach box. As a mother tucks her baby into its cot, she tucked me into the box, and away we went.

We were the first to try this winter trail, so Norman and his team went ahead of us over the first bay. Every few feet he stopped and sounded the ice with his hatchet. It proved to be safe, so he shouted back, "O.K. Come ahead." We caught up to him and when we reached the far side of the bay, he waved his whip, turned homeward, and our dogs bolted forward.

It was extremely hard work for Mr. Brown and the dogs to break trail over lakes and portages, through underbrush and over rocks. He would run beside the dogs, urging and encouraging them, sometimes waist deep in light snow, then, panting, perspiring, and exhausted, he would flop back onto the komatic and mush with one foot to push and shove the komatic forward over treacherous, frozen, rocky, and stumpy mounds.

I had wired the telegraph operator at Mutton Bay to find out if the last wide expanse of dangerous bay was frozen enough to hold us. I was informed that it was safe. Through some error in translating from English to French and back again to English, the message had been misinterpreted. It should have been, "Not safe to hold." One little word omitted from the telegram made a lot of difference.

At one o'clock Sunday afternoon, we reached the head of this bay. In front of us, instead of a sheet of ice, there stretched a quarter of a mile of open water. It was too late to return to Whale Head and there was no shelter in the vicinity, so we unhitched the dogs, cached the komatic, blankets, and coach box and started hiking. Even in summer this is a long, hard trek, because there is no trail. Now deep banks of light snow, icy rocks, open crevices between the rocks with slob ice at the bottom, and thick underbrush made it twenty times more difficult and treacherous. At any moment we might step on what appeared to be a soft snowbank and sink into an open chasm which extended many feet downward between the rocks and ended in deep water. We had to face it because tomorrow would not be any better. Both of us preferred the trek to lighting a fire and walking around all night to keep from freezing.

We left everything but my medical bag and an axe and set out. At times we floundered waist deep and had difficulty getting a footing to crawl out. Mr. Brown used his axe as a fastening hook in the ice. He would pull himself across a chasm, haul himself up the other side, then reach down and swing me across to safety. In other places, he would grasp a root of underbrush on the opposite side of a crevice and cut holes for his toes so that, inch by inch, he could crawl up. Then he would seize my extended wrists and drag me up beside him. In several places the underbrush was so thick he had to cut a trail through. It would have taken fifteen minutes to reach the Station by dog-team over the ice. Hiking, it took us nearly three hours. Almost exhausted, hungry as a starving wolf, and, perhaps, just a little fed up with the Coast, I plodded behind Mr. Brown to the Station at four o'clock.

How we enjoyed our hot supper!

When the enormous amount of calories consumed began to produce their magic energy, new life coursed through my whole being. Before tackling the waiting mass of neglected work, sleep and cleanliness were essential. I stepped out of woollens donned fifteen days before, lathered, scrubbed, and polished my body until it glowed. With a clean body, fresh clothes, and a satisfied stomach, I was ready for anything.

ONLY three days were left to get ready for the Mission tree and Christmas Day. It had been the custom of the previous Mission nurse to prepare the tree, presents, and candy. Invalids and shut-ins received special presents, and some homes, where there were a number of small children and not much income, received a Christmas dinner.

A homesick maid had greeted me and wanted to leave the next morning. Finally she agreed to help clean up the place and remain until I could train another girl. In the hope that it might cheer June, I told her to get a gang of girls for Monday morning and we would wade back to the woods and cut our own tree. This gave her new interest and by night we had the tree and the Christmas spirit filled the air.

The concert and tree festivities were much as they had been in other years. The people were more prosperous, the presents perhaps a little more desirable, but the lovely spirit of Christmas was just the same.

On Christmas Day we had a schoolteacher, his wife and two children, as well as a former schoolteacher, her husband and little boy as our guests. This was the first real Christmas dinner ever eaten by one of the maids and the first time she had seen a Christmas tree or attended such a concert. It was a joy, yet pathetic, to hear her exclamations of delight and awe at the dinner and the tree with all its trimmings. I began to wonder about our Christianity. She was twenty years old, living in a Christian province. I am sorry to say that there are many girls and boys, and some men and women, who have never seen Christmas trees nor shared in the thought and spirit that goes with them.

On the fifteenth of March a Labrador blizzard had somewhat abated when Uncle John came to the Station with a wire. "Robert has had an accident. Get a team and come at once. Our team will meet you halfway."

Once more I drew on my heavy woollens, collected a few emergency instruments, bandages, disinfectant, and sedatives and was ready. The gale that had raged all night had made the trail a series of snow-ridge waves. The dogs would bound into the soft banks, wallow through until the komatic balanced half over the ridge, where it paused in mid-air. Then, from the snow-peak wave, we would take a header into the feathery snow. It was difficult for the dogs to make much headway. Soon their tongues hung out and every few feet one, then another, would swerve aside, lap some cooling snow, then race on. Halfway to our destination we met the other team coming for me. Uncle John advised us to have the two teams mush side by side so that I could ride first with one, then the other. This lessened the continuous drag for each team. As soon as the dogs felt the weight lighten they spurted ahead and we made much better time. Each driver knelt on his komatic and mushed with his free leg, which gave the komatic a forward shove and kept it in rhythmic motion.

Confusion and excitement greeted us. Mrs. Peters, her apron and arms spattered with blood, stood outside on the porch twisting a bloodstained cloth. Inside, the neighbors stood about, whispering and talking in excited voices. "It be wonderfully bad!" "Will he live?" "How did it happen?" "See his cap!" "Look at the torn leather." Then came a dead silence followed by, "Sh-h, Sister's here!"

I took one look at Robert and tried to get some coherent information about the accident. "The windcharger split open his head," shouted Mr. Armer. "No, he ripped it open as he fell off the roof," shouted Mr. Thoms. "I don't believe it because he was not unconscious when he crawled down. Look at the trail of blood. That proves it," asserted Mr. Armer. "Listen, Sister," spoke up Mr. Wells, "a windcharger certainly split his head."

I went to Robert, who was lying fully clothed with a cold wet towel across his forehead. The front of his sweater was a gory mass, for he had crawled through the snow while bleeding. When I raised the towel, a sickening sight met my eyes. His whole scalp had been ripped open to the bone. Around the gaping wound, blood-matted hair stuck fast. I laid the towel back on his head and wrote a wire to the doctor pleading with him to come, but, in my heart, I knew it was impossible to expect him. While waiting for a reply, I began to rack my brains to recall skull surgery witnessed in the operating room.

The reply from the doctor came: "Go ahead."

I had never tackled such a wound, but there was no way out of it. I recalled that it was not advisable to give an anæsthetic to uncertain skull cases except in extreme emergencies, and especially without a doctor available. Fortunately, I had brought a bottle of green soap. With soap and razor I cut away as much of the matted hair as possible, thus delaying as long as possible the suturing operation. I taxed my brain to recall surgical details, and tried to fortify myself physically and spiritually.

When I had clipped away the hair I had to take small forceps and pick out, piece by piece, the frayed shreds from his old leather cap, which had been driven deep into the wound and which adhered to the bare skull.

I then set up a primitive operating room. Robert watched me as I worked. When I was ready to suture the wound I asked, "What about it?" "Go ahead," he replied. He certainly had a tough scalp. He gave no indication of fear at the next move. As I pulled suture after suture through his tough skin, occasionally he twisted his shoulders or his facial muscles twitched. But, to my enquiries, "Can you stand it?" always he replied, "Go ahead." The courage and grit of these fishermen would put most of us to shame.

When I had finished I tucked him in bed and gave him a strong sedative. He was our mail carrier, a thin, wiry man constantly exposed to sun and winds, and his face had become almost as brown and tanned as sealskin. No weather, if it were possible to travel, would prevent him having his mail on time. Conscientious, friendly, and obliging he had many times given up the comforts of his boat and komatic to give some passenger a lift to the next village or to rush a patient to the hospital. He was accustomed to sleeping sitting up, on a hard floor with a mailbag for a pillow, curled up in soaking wet clothing over a smoking fire, or even on the snow under an upturned boat. I knew sleep would soothe him, but I wondered, with trepidation, if nature would assist my attempts to prevent infection.

Two days afterward word came through that he was feeling fine. Several days later a dog-team whizzed past the Station window and I heard the driver shout "Halt!" Could I be mistaken? No, it was Robert and he had driven his team six miles in order to have his dressing changed!

The first Sunday in April I had settled in a comfortable chair for a little relaxation when I heard a loud pounding on the outer door. What now? I thought, and shouted, "Come in." The door opened, letting in a gust of wind and snow, followed by a strapping, stalwart fisherman muffled in heavy woollens and dickie. I knew by the expression on his face that some accident had sent him. He stepped over the threshold, closed the door and said, "My mother has been thrown from a komatic. I think her leg is broken. I have come for yous." He was a stranger so I asked, "Who is your mother?" "Aunt Lucy," he replied. I knew Aunt Lucy, mother and aunt to three villages. She was more than sixty years old but often travelled night and day over rocks, waded through slush, mud, and slob, jumped on and off komatics, clung to boats, and wallowed through snow to reach some expectant mother, then sat up twelve or twenty-four hours waiting for the baby. I shuddered as I thought of this efficient, tall, heavy woman with a broken leg.

I threw together the necessary equipment and drew on layers of woollens. All the time my mind kept jumping ahead. Would there be any way of getting her to a doctor? But having learned never to borrow trouble until trouble walked across my path, I decided to enjoy the komatic drive. It was an ideal day and we sped quickly over ice and snow, up hills, through gorges, dodged between underbrush and around ballacaters, then just missed an open glade as we bolted out onto a sheet of glare ice.

I found Mrs. Pry, a neighbor, weeping behind her apron. Mrs. Gray, Aunt Lucy's daughter-in-law, was holding Aunt Lucy's leg and doing her utmost to keep her comfortable but she was suffering excruciating pain. They had managed to get her to a bumpy couch in the kitchen. I stripped off an outer layer of clothing and gently lifted her leg, which swung inward. She screamed at the slightest movement. It was evident that her hip-bone was broken. We went out and unearthed a suitable board for an improvised splint. Darkness had settled in, making travel impossible. Besides, the telegraph office had closed for the night. All I could do was try to make her comfortable until the following morning.

It was the worst time of the year for travel; komatic roads had broken and ice still blocked the harbors, making boat travel impossible. To get her to a doctor or hospital we would have to travel thirty-six miles behind dogs over rough hills. It was quite possible that no komatic would stand the strain over the bare moss, frozen hubbles, and the jumps over open glades. At best it would take at least two days and if a storm came on suddenly we might be stranded in some tiny, isolated fishing shack for days or weeks.

At daybreak, I sent Mr. Gray over the trail to the telegraph office with a wire. Fortunately, the doctor was at home and an answer came back much more quickly than I had anticipated. "Wait until you hear from me." Shortly afterward a second message came saying, "An R.C.A.F. plane is patrolling the Coast. The pilot has volunteered to come back for you. Be ready in an hour." From the bottom of my heart I was thankful for doctors and pilots. I knew the doctor would leave no stone unturned to get help to us, but I had no knowledge that a plane was in that vicinity. Known and loved from one end of the Coast to the other, the doctor, like a ferret, smelled help when there was a need and usually got it in time.

Always energetic and active, never having been sick, Aunt Lucy had a dread of hospitals. During the night we had suggested that she go to a hospital if possible. She had raised all kinds of objections. Now that a way was open an immediate decision had to be made. Her son settled the problem. "She goes." Suffering excruciating pain, she did not reply.

Hardly had we received the telegram, when we heard the whir of a plane overhead. We were not ready. Usually fisherfolk take their own time, but in emergencies they can work quickly. John jumped to get the stretcher, fell over a chair, stepped on the puppy's tail, and sprawled across the kitchen table. As if in a daze, grandpa walked about, muttering to himself, "What'll Ise do when herns gone?" Mary grabbed a blanket and started to muffle Aunt Lucy's head. No doubt she thought the speed of the plane would blow her head off.

More confusion followed as John exclaimed, "How will wese

get hern out—the door is narrower than the stretcher?" Someone shouted, "Uncork her." "Who, uncork who?" yelled John. "The outside door, mother corked it last fall." In a few moments yards of pasted cloth covering was ripped off the door sills. By the time the door was widened we had Aunt Lucy safely roped to the homemade stretcher, then men passed the stretcher through the door to others, who carried it to the komatic and drew the komatic to the edge of the ice. By this time the plane was circling overhead. Since this was an educational experience the teacher dismissed the children so that they could be there for the excitement. They added considerably to the noise and confusion. Several small children were wailing loudly, others shouted excitedly while getting underfoot and falling about in the snow.

Suddenly shouts went up, "Look, herns a heading away!" "Herns leaving us!" "Hern can't make it!" My heart sank. I thought how we had coaxed Aunt Lucy until finally she had not objected to riding in the plane—although she had not consented —and I still wondered if she would refuse to go when the plane actually landed. I held my breath and waited. Though suffering and terrified at the thought of a hospital and a plane ride, she now saw her only means of transportation fading away and commenced weeping bitterly.

Once more a wave of excitement rippled through the crowd. "Herns coming back!" "Herns coming down!" "Herns going to make it!"

Like a huge eagle, the plane swooped down near the ice, made a quick dive, then skimmed straight for us. Men, women, and children screamed and scattered in all directions to make way for this improvised bird-ambulance. A few hundred feet from us, the motor gave one last turn and the plane glided to a stop directly in front of Aunt Lucy. She was such a tiny, pathetic speck beside the great machine. I felt extremely sorry for her and yearned to comfort her as the men lifted her, stretcher and all, into the waiting plane. Weeping women sobbed farewells as I crawled in beside the pilot. The engineer closed the plane door and a new world opened for Aunt Lucy while a feeling of sorrow and loss settled over the village. She was their midwife, mother, aunt, and general comforter. Would she ever return?

In less than twenty-five minutes we were coming down over the hospital, thirty-six miles away. Previously over the same route with another case, it had taken me four and a half days, with three boats, three dog-teams, and several hours hiking to cover the same distance.

More people awaited us on the ice at Harrington than we had left in Aunt Lucy's home village. The doctor, another R.C.A.F. pilot, relatives, and friends stood gazing skyward. We glided down into their midst.

Thoughtlessly, thinking I was stepping from an ambulance, I jumped to the ground and stepped ahead of the plane. Shouts assailed me from all sides, "Sister! Take care, the propeller!" The doctor grabbed my arm and pulled me backward. Afterward I realized my danger when he told me that if I had stepped six inches nearer my head would have been instantly severed from my body. When this excitement had subsided, eager hands grabbed the komatic ropes and drew Aunt Lucy to the hospital. An X ray confirmed my diagnosis, and soon the patient was in a comfortable hospital bed, with doctor and nurses to care for her.

In a few months Aunt Lucy was back on the job "borning babies" and managing the whole village.

I was very happy about Aunt Lucy and, as one of the neighbors called the plane, "the miracle from the sky" that had made her stay in hospital possible. Yet I realized that it was not at all likely that such plane service for the sick would become commonplace in Mutton Bay and the surrounding area. The landings are too hazardous. The old reliable dog-teams and boats will still have to be used and there will always be plenty of work for the resident nurse.

THE people with whom I worked were an unending source of interest to me. When I thought I knew one of my patients or the parents of the children I nursed fairly well, something would often happen to change the picture.

I had not much use for Peter Smith. Shiftless, lazy, ignorant, he could hardly write his name, yet he doggedly refused to exert himself to supply one cord of wood so that his little daughters could attend school. His wife, Bella, was his slave, yet she worshipped him. Many times the family barely had enough to keep body and soul together but still they managed to struggle on.

One day the other side of Peter's nature came to the foreground. His little three-year-old girl, Nancy, became seriously ill. Peter was away on a three-day trip down the Coast and there was a rough sea. Since she was a tuberculosis patient, I knew the only hope, if any, was an immediate operation. The steamer came into the harbor and Bella gave me permission to take her to Harrington to the hospital and doctor. I sent a wire asking operators along the Coast to try and get in touch with Peter. As soon as he received the message he jumped into his boat and for two days and a night, without rest or food, he battled the waves. He arrived at Harrington in time to see Nancy before she was called to her last home.

Two days later Peter came to see if I would bring my camera and take a snapshot of his little girl. This tiny, angel-faced babe was dressed in her Sunday white dress, lying propped up in a sitting position on a small table. She looked so fragile and sweet he wanted to remember her like this.

Tender hearts are often covered by hard-shelled coverings. I had more respect for Peter after that incident. On the other hand, had he been more thoughtful and a better provider probably today he would have a living instead of a picture Nancy.

I grieved over little Nancy. Her life and death seemed to stand for the almost insuperable difficulties with which the Labrador nurse must contend. At times, of course, I could rejoice when I remembered the other side of the picture—the patients whom I had been able to help, the wonderful work of the hospital at Harrington Harbour.

I was nearing the end of my term at Mutton Bay, had in fact overstayed my time because of the continued scarcity of nurses, and I was tired. But like everyone else in the village, I was thrilled one hot July day to hear the good news that the salmon were running up-river to spawn. This was gold for the fishermen.

I had never seen the salmon going upstream and I decided to refresh my jaded body and mind by taking a day off to see the sight. So I went with Mr. Vassey as he rowed his boat alongside the nets to gather in his salmon harvest. Fascinated, I watched those beautiful silvery bodies glistening in the sun as they flopped and splashed in the nets. But I could not help but feel that it was a cruel business.

The two men grabbed the net, raised it above the boat, then carefully slipped the net from under the salmon's gills and dropped the flapping fish into the bottom of the boat. When all the salmon were removed from the net we returned to the fishing stage where the finishing process was at once begun. Again I stood fascinated as I watched those expert men and women at the age-old trade. The first man slashed off heads, ripped up bellies, tore out entrails, then flopped the fish over to the cleaner, who dragged the body to the edge of the water and gave it the final cleaning under salt water. When the fish was thoroughly cleaned, he hung it on pegs in the cool canning room. Later, the cutter slashed each salmon into pieces and passed each piece to the packer, who packed the flesh into the tins and weighed them. This systematic, quick, efficient passing of salmon from the boat to the cans was marvellous to behold. The last man flipped on the paper tops and passed the tins to the crimper, who pressed the tin covers in place and crimped them. The crimper carried the tins to the bath and started stoking. Every tin had hours of continuous boiling and then stood on its side on the cool grass until thoroughly cold before being packed in the final case for shipment. Each case contained forty-eight one-pound tins of salmon. Later, these would be sold to the highest bidder.

A day or so later I had an unexpected thrill when I strolled up the river to the rapids to do a little trout fishing. As I drew near the rapids, I watched the salmon that had escaped the nets splashing in the pools at the bottom of the falls. Suddenly a flashing streak of shimmering silver would leap from the lower rapids, straight up, clear the roaring, rushing rapids and swim away above them.

As I stood there, up shot a beautiful, glistening streak. But this salmon had underestimated its strength and was carried sideways and fell, panting and exhausted, on the flat rock at the edge of the water. Tired by the long struggle, it remained there gasping as if stunned, then it raised its head and commenced to flop about in an attempt to get back to the cool water. But it was doomed, for I knew I would have that prize. Never before had I seen such a fish on shore, alive, and waiting to be taken. I dropped my trout rod and line and made a quick dash for the unfortunate, helpless victim. I forgot everything, even the danger of slipping into the treacherous rapids or of being bitten by the salmon. Until I grabbed this one I never realized the power of a salmon. It fought like a tiger and when I jumped onto its back it bucked like a bronco. Never before had I thought of a salmon as having strength. Always it had been flesh to eat. Now I understood how it was possible for those fish to force their way up the rapids to their spawning grounds. It bucked and fought a battle of wit and strength as I clung to its slippery back. At last, the powerful strokes of the tail became weaker. Covered with blood and slime, perspiring and wet from the flying spray, I was nearly exhausted; but I had the satisfaction of seeing that magnificent fish flop, once, twice, three times, then remain still, panting, but with no more fight in it. Although I was the conqueror I did not gloat over a fish that had put up such a gallant battle.

Too tired to move, I sat on its back, then slid off onto the rocks, but still held firmly to its gills. If it gave a final flop and swam away in its native waters, I should have only a doubtful fish story to tell. As I sat there instinct told me that something was missing. I looked at my arm and saw that my watch was not on it. For a moment I wondered if my prize was worth this loss. However, I spied the watch in a pool of water near the rapids and was able to capture it—none the worse for its bath.

The salmon, as I knew, was my prize but not my fish because I did not have a license to fish for salmon. All rights of that river belonged to Mr. Vassey, who had a salmon cannery a quarter of a mile away. Between the cannery and me there were rocky ledges, underbrush, and treacherous paths over which I needed both feet, hands, and eyes to climb to safety. I did not dare leave this beauty to go for help because if I did it might be spirited away and I would think it was all a dream.

My clothes were a mass of gore and slime. I cupped some water in my hands and took off the thickest of it. At best, I looked as though I had been fighting a bloody battle. With my fingers fastened in the gills of the big fish and my line and rod over my shoulder, I set off over the winding trail. Every few feet I had to ease the salmon to the ground and take a breathing spell. Finally I reached the cannery. Mr. Vassey was certain that the salmon would weigh fifteen to seventeen pounds. He was as surprised as I was; he had been a fisherman for forty years and had never heard of such a thing happening before. I began to think I really had a fish story.

Mr. Vassey removed the head, fins, tail, and entrails and canned my salmon. It made eleven pounds of delicious eating and must have made a feast for many people, but I did not get a taste of it. The sport of catching it offset the loss of eating it, and the day's outing helped me through the last part of a twenty-six month stretch of continuous duty.

On one of the last mornings, as I stood in my office replenishing my medical kit before starting out on my morning visits, I heard the maid say, "She be in her office. Go right in." Footsteps shook the whole building. A giant-size man filled the doorway. His huge broad shoulders, bulging muscles, and fat chin stubbled with reddish-brown whiskers gave him the appearance of a cave man. As he stepped through the door, he hauled off his worn, greasy, peaked cap and boomed, "Good-morning, Sister."

I recognized powerful, quick-tempered, big-hearted Red John from across the tickle.

He lowered his huge frame to the one small chair. Silence ensued until I asked, "What's the trouble?"

"The missus sent me for yous," he said almost softly as he shook his head from side to side feelingly, then continued, "Our Janey be wonderful sick and she be crying. She can't cough and her kinkorn will not glutch. Me, I hates to see the helpless little thing suffering so."

As we hurried through the kitchen door Red John stooped down and said, "Let me take your bag, Sister."

I looked up at him and felt like Tom Thumb gazing up at a giant and wondered how I would ever keep up with those powerful, long strides.

We set out over the rocks. Ten feet ahead of me he looked back, waited until I caught up to him, changed his pace to mine, and we went on.

I recalled how Red John had boasted to the village people, "Wese never call Sister. Ise has no use for her newfangled ideas."

I must not make a mistake in my treatment or diagnosis. As we strode along I uttered a little prayer for guidance ending with "O God, if it be Thy will, save her."

Maggie, Red John's wife, sat rocking Janey, who was stretched across her lap, gasping for breath, trying to cry, trying to cough, and unable to do anything as she stiffened out in fear.

A thorough examination showed no mucous film of diphtheria. There were no symptoms of that fatal disease, croup. No history of deceiving whooping cough was encountered. In order not to lose a finger, I placed a clothespin between Janey's teeth, crooked my finger, and ran it along the tonsil area, then to the tongue. There it encountered a two-pronged pinlike obstacle. The child spluttered, choked, and kicked frantically. Red John leaped forward, grabbed my arm, and bellowed, "Yous choking hern." He jerked my arm back. Out came my finger and with it a V-shaped fishbone. As the bone fell to the floor, Janey sat up, coughed, spat out a small gog of mucous and blood. Then, from relief or as if she thought we were playing a game, she wiggled her toes, put up her arms, and began to coo at us.

Red John looked at me and faltered, "Ise didn't mean to butt in, Sister, but Ise thought she was dying and I loves her so." He bent his huge shoulders forward. Little Janey entwined her wee arms around that great neck. He raised her face to his and stood tenderly holding her as she slobbered kisses on his cheek.

When I left Maggie said, "Sister, Ise glad I thought to send for yous. Come in whenever yous are going by."

At the wharf, when Red John left me, all he said was "Sister, Ise guess wese needs yous here in Mutton Bay . . . I likes my family so much Ise would hate to lose Janey. She is so cuddly."

His words of thanks were few but there was no doubt as to their sincerity and they warmed my heart.

The last week in July I received a letter from our secretary informing me that relief would reach me so that I could leave on the steamer early in August.

Physically I was in need of a rest and a holiday. Yet when the last day came and good-byes must be said, I was loathe to leave. When the packing was done and the last of my callers had gone, I sat on our back porch to watch, for perhaps the last time, the afterglow of a magnificent Labrador sunset. Some of the peace of that lovely evening stole into my heart and I thought not of the hardships of life on the Coast nor of the tragedies I had witnessed, but of the fine people I had come to know—their free and independent spirit, their enjoyment of simple pleasures, their patience and courage, their unselfish helpfulness in time of trouble, their faith in God and their desire to do His will.

I had planned a very different life for myself and when the call came that Mutton Bay needed me, the decision was not an easy one to make. But I was glad, very glad, that I had had these years here; I had come to love this harsh yet beautiful land and the reserved yet friendly people I had served to the best of my ability. As I sat musing I remembered the words of a homesick lad who had gone from Mutton Bay to Montreal. Much had been done for him; he was living in what was luxury compared to his Coast home and yet he was unhappy. One day he was wandering by the water front when he happened to meet a former Grenfell worker. When she asked him how he liked living in the big city, his pent-up feelings found relief in words that she could not forget—they went something like this: "Oh 't is all right . . . and I make good money now, and I can send some home to help the young 'uns . . . but I dunno . . . At home the ducks and birds will be coming in from the sea . . . the trout will be leaping in the streams . . . the salmon will be coming up the river . . . the fish will be running in the deep water. I can see a seal near a cake of ice and I am not there to shoot it. . . . I miss the smell of the sea, the smell of the fish, our northern lights. . . . I miss the howl of the dogs at bedtime and coming home at night, the neighbors asking, 'How many fish today?' Here, in the city, you have everything, but 't is so dirty, so noisy, and so crowded. . . . People are always in a hurry . . . and they don't care what you're doing. . . . I like it better up north."

And I knew with complete certainty that when I reached the big city with its noise and bustle and hurry I should often feel like this homesick lad, for I, too, "like it better up north."

THE END